INSOLVENCY EXPLAINED

Bankruptcies, Assignments, Bulk Transfers, Receiverships, Probates, and Workouts

David J. Cook

Cover by Jill Tedhams/ABA Publishing.

The materials contained herein represent the opinions of the authors and editors, and should not be construed to be the views or opinions of the law firms or companies with whom such persons are in partnership with, associated with, or employed by, nor of the American Bar Association or the General Practice, Solo and Small Firm Division unless adopted pursuant to the bylaws of the Association.

Nothing contained in this book is to be considered as the rendering of legal advice for specific cases, and readers are responsible for obtaining such advice from their own legal counsel. This book is intended for educational and informational purposes only.

Printed in the United States of America.

20 19 18 17   5 4 3 2 1

Library of Congress Cataloging-in-Publication Data

Names: Cook, David J., 1949– author.
Title: Insolvency explained / David Cook.
Description: Chicago : American Bar Association, 2017.
Identifiers: LCCN 2016049813 (print) ┃ LCCN 2016050238 (ebook) ┃ ISBN
   9781634255639 (print) ┃ ISBN 9781634255646 (ePub)
Subjects: LCSH: Bankruptcy—United States. ┃ Debtor and creditor—United
   States.
Classification: LCC KF1524 .C6346 2017 (print) ┃ LCC KF1524 (ebook) ┃ DDC
   346.7307/8—dc23
LC record available at https://lccn.loc.gov/2016049813

Discounts are available for books ordered in bulk. Special consideration is given to state bars, CLE programs, and other bar-related organizations. Inquire at ABA Publishing, American Bar Association, 321 North Clark Street, Chicago, Illinois 60654-7598.

www.ShopABA.org

Contents

Preface

This book covers lots of ground. Insolvency incorporates bankruptcy, which is federal law, and assignments for the benefit of creditors, bulk sales, receiverships, workouts, and probates, which are creatures of state law. Victim and licensee funds, bonds, and uninsured workers' compensation funds are creatures of both federal and state law.

Most of the law discussed in this book is available online. Having a copy of the bankruptcy code at hand can be helpful but is not required. Referring to Article 9 of the Uniform Commercial Code likewise can be helpful. (The bankruptcy code, bankruptcy rules, and the entirety of the Uniform Commercial Code are online.) Many attorneys offer helpful online articles that explain the minutiae of bankruptcy and the Uniform Commercial Code. The United States Bankruptcy Court (N.D. CA) offers an online, well organized summary of case law.

This book offers you insight into what is *not* in written in the law.

An overarching theme of this book is that a secured creditor who has properly filed (or recorded) the financing statement might well survive any challenge in an insolvency proceeding and even emerge unscathed. Consider an unavoidable security to be the life preserver that enables the creditor to quietly drift away from the sinking ship. A secured creditor includes a creditor who has obtained an interest in the debtor's property by virtue of a consensual lien (UCC filing), or non consensual lien (judgment or attachment lien or levy).

This book discusses bulk sales, which are the statutory procedure for the sale of a business and are found in Article 6 of the UCC. Many states have repealed or modified Article 6, which might seem to render this discussion somewhat moot. However, California has retained the bulk sales act. Given California's status as a major marketplace, familiarity with Article 6 can be helpful. Again, a perfected security interest protects the creditor because the buyer, arising from a bulk sale, takes subject to the filed lien. Given multistate practice and retail stores domiciled in many jurisdictions, knowledge of the bulk sales act is a necessity.

This book also discusses probates, which are virtually creatures of state law—and particularly the state probate code. While states might offer differing probate code, many states follow the Uniform Probate Code. Likewise, these proceedings do not trump, but take subject to, a valid security interest. In addition, this book discusses workouts, which consist of payment programs, extensions, pot plans, and discounts.

The Cocktail of Insolvency and the Fair Debt Collection Practice Acts (Federal and State)

In the 9th Circuit, the major decision is *In Chaussee* 399 B.R. 225 (9th Circuit, BAP, 2008), a BAP decision that holds that the FDCPA does not apply in bankruptcy proceedings. The summary of this decision is that the bankruptcy court is "self policing for [creditor] abuse."

In the 3rd Circuit, the circuit court held that the FDCPA does apply in bankruptcy court. See *Simon vs. FIA Car Svcs.* 732 F. 3rd. 259 (3rd Circuit, 2013). The summary of this decision is that the federal FDCPA can and should be applied without any disruption to bankruptcy court proceedings. The debtor claimed that the proof of claim was for a stale debt, which is a practice (i.e., time barred debts) prohibited under the FDCPA. The attorney filed the proof of claim. The circuits are in conflict, which will be resolved at some point in time. Given that this is an unsettled area of the law in some circuits, further research is in high order.

FDCPA cases fill the federal dockets of all circuits. Compliance with the FDCPA is a big deal because the attorney (you, my reader) is personally liable for a violation. An attorney is a debt collector, says the Supreme Court in *Heintz v. Jenkins*, 514 U.S. 291 (1995). There is no greater shock for most attorneys than to see their names as defendants in *federal* lawsuits because they left a phone message on the debtor's residential answering machine. Window envelopes, which might reveal the name of the creditor or an account number, can also launch federal lawsuits.

In many cases, the damages in most FDCPA cases might be nominal, but the attorney's fees can be substantial. Anecdotal evidence suggests that FDCPA cases are fee machines, which early settlement or a well managed Rule 68 offer might bring to timely conclusion. Worse, many consumer collection attorneys engage in a volume practice, which invites a *federal* class action lawsuit. Six figures for costs are common in these cases. Let's keep in mind that the FDCPA bars improper letters, envelopes, misleading or incorrect demands, requires Mini-Miranda warnings, requires great specificity in lawsuits and letters, prohibits third party disclosures, and has other strict requirements. States offer their own parallel FDCPA acts, which might impose liability upon the creditor and might even offer a wider range of damages than the federal FDCPA. Getting back to the question: Are attorneys liable for FDCPA transgressions that occur in bankruptcy court? The answer to this question is "maybe" and "depends" and "more likely than not." Expect that at a future point in time, the Supreme Court will have to sort out this problem.

Introduction: Insolvency Is a Settled Expectation

Find What You Need Quickly

The mantra of every attorney, business person, financial professional, collection agent, and banker is "What do I need to know?" Without an attorney who cycles through insolvencies as a part of a practice, quickly assessing the filing or other requirement for many professionals is burdensome.

This is the "Tell Me What I Need to Know" book. It is organized into two major sections.

- The first section is a general discussion of insolvency and the requirements that are common in each type of proceedings. Every insolvency proceeding has its own claim requirements, distribution procedures, risk of claim objections, and nuances that must be tackled. This first section offers a general overview to enable the reader to better eyeball what is truly important.
- The second section looks at each type of insolvency. The headings of each section provide the step by step overview.

Given each type of insolvency is a standalone process, the reader can quickly find the section relevant to his or her needs, as opposed to wading, page by page and chapter by chapter, through an entire tome. When faced with a bankruptcy—whether as a creditor or as a debtor—the reader wants to quickly learn the law of bankruptcy and, just as importantly, ignore the law of bulk transfers, although it is highly entertaining.

Following the opening section of each topic is a discussion of the key touchstones of each proceeding. Few practitioners care about fee applications in bankruptcy court, which is certainly a more important topic for fee applicants. However, sales orders are important in bankruptcy, as we learn in the General Motors case (the ignition switch case). On the other hand, every practitioner becomes immersed in timely filing a proof of claim, complying with the automatic stay, and learning how to defend a preference lawsuit (in bankruptcy court). These topics of discussion are the hit parade.

The unbendable rule, whether you wish to plaster it on a T-shirt, carve it in the marble mantle of the court, or offer it in a Chinese fortune cookie, is this: File the proof of claim on time. Everything else follows suit. Consider the timely filed proof of claim the stakeholder. Under bankruptcy law, a filed proof of claim is deemed allowed unless an objection is filed. A filed proof of claim, in any proceedings, offers recognizable standing in any ensuing litigation.

Approaching Insolvency Requires Prompt Action

The core of most insolvency is that a third party intervenes in, and reorders, the relationship between the debtor and creditor. The "third party" is usually a bankruptcy trustee, chapter debtor in possession, assignee for the benefit of creditors, or equity receiver, all of whom have statutory rights to set aside a transaction, sue to recover prior payments, and topple improperly perfected (or nonexistent) security interests. The role of the third party is to marshal assets for the benefit of the unsecured creditors. Errors are easy to make: failure to record a UCC filing with the county recorder to reach real property improvements (i.e., fixtures, leasehold interests [a long term lease], trade fixtures, etc.) or the failure to file the financing statement with the U.S. Copyright office to reach a copyright (filing with the secretary of state will not reach a copyright). Other common errors are the failure to do a search through the secretary of state in name of the predecessor entity to the debtor, failure to do a search post transaction to insure that the financing statement actually filed timely and without the risk of any intervening liens, and even the failure to confirm the correct legal name, identity, or structure (i.e., corporation or LLC) of the debtor.

Time is usually an enemy and rarely a friend. Bankruptcy trustees can "claw back" (i.e., recover) transfers, payments, liens, or levies which took place within 90 days prior to the filing of the petition. A trustee can reach insider transactions that go back one year and even further to reach fraudulent conveyances. When a debtor defaults, counsel needs to first look downstream for the pending insolvency proceedings. In the age of sailing, lookouts perched high in the crow's nest could always spot the mast of the approaching vessel rising over the horizon. Few insolvencies are a surprise. If the debtor is a public entity and files disclosure with the Securities & Exchange Commission, these disclosures appear on the SEC website EDGAR, which consists of accountants' opinions that express "doubts about the entity continuing as a going concern." General Motors broadcast its pending bankruptcy through its EDGAR filings.

Here is a more detailed survey of common substantive errors that accrue in the shadow of approaching insolvency proceedings:

A. Failure to prosecute state prejudgment remedies that would insure the secured status of a creditor's claim, outside the 90 day preference period, and enhance manifold payment through the proceedings. Failure to timely file or record attachment liens. Failure to recover property subject to a security interest, lease, conditional sales contract, or other lien. The risk here is that the collateral might "take flight," or suffer vandalism, or damage, which renders the security interest valueless. Failure to timely file, perfect, or record judgment liens. In some states (i.e., California) the service of a debtor's examination order imposes a lien on all personal property, which might survive a bankruptcy, or assigned, if perfected beyond 90 days.

B. Failure to properly perfect a security interest in the debtor's property, including the failure to file or record a UCC (financing statement), or file (or record) with the correct filing agency. A security interest might be subject to recording (not filing) the financing statement with the county recorder. Many leases, credit applications, sales contracts, invoices, or other commercial documents contain a security interest which the client has not yet perfected.

C. Failure to repossess collateral in the hands of the debtor or third party when reasonably available, and without breach of peace. The act of repossession mitigates the risk of theft, vandalism, and damage and, better yet, acts to perfect the secured creditor's security interest.

D. Failure to properly recognize a security interest which resides in a lease, credit application, contract, or terms and conditions and timely perfect the security by filing and recording with the UCC.

E. Failure to prosecute reclamation rights, rights to suspend performance, or right to recall products in transit. This includes the failure to prosecute these rights in a bankruptcy proceeding. Failure to advise the client to cease sales on a credit basis and convert the relationship to C.O.D. or stop sales altogether.

F. Failure to carefully consider a steeply discounted cash offer of settlement and recommend acceptance if the cash offer is more than the probable recovery from an insolvency proceeding and free of any potential "claw back" as a preference. ("A bird is hand is worth more than two in the bush.")

G. Failure to recognize that the customer (or vendor) is failing, or even that it has already filed Chapter 11 or 13 proceedings which are currently ongoing (which can be found via a search through PACER or commercial services such as D&B). Finding out that a customer is in the midst of a Chapter 11 or 13 is a surprise. Getting paid from a debtor for a post petition debt during the midst of a Chapter 11 might require the filing of a motion to compel the administrative debt, or allowance thereof. The debtor might well oppose the motion. The court might grant administrative status but order payment upon plan confirmation that might never come about, or cycle through months (or more) of bankruptcy litigation. (Note: Many debtors pay post petition debts on time, lest the creditor seek an order converting the case to a Chapter 7 based on the debtor's mismanagement.)

H. Failure to demand as part of a forbearance agreement additional collateral or guarantors or to review the transaction to insure that the security was properly documented or perfected. When the debtor defaults, counsel should "start from scratch" to insure that the original loan, credit, or prior workout agreement was correctly drafted and implemented and that the security interest was not only perfected, but that a professional search was undertaken to insure the position of the security. If the parties at the outset negotiated for a first lien, but given a default downstream, the creditor might be shocked to learn that the first position was illusory given intervening liens, levies, and even transfers. The fact that the debtor defaults under a workout is symptomatic a wider range of defaults of obligations owed to other creditors. A default is harbinger of a probable bankruptcy or other insolvency.

This list of potential errors is illustrative but not exhaustive. It teaches that in the face of a brewing insolvency, counsel should take a highly proactive role to mitigate the client's potential loss. The main objective in these scenarios is to convert the creditor from unsecured to secured, which enhances any prospect of recovery.

1

What Is Insolvency?

Insolvency is a general term for any legal proceeding or business arrangement that enables a failed or troubled business to seek to liquidate its assets, pay its creditors, and terminate or reorganize its business operation. A legal proceeding establishes a court appointed trustee, or even a debtor in possession, who has a brand new set of legal rights and powers that can vacate or nullify state court judgments; void key contract provisions; stay enforcement of valid liens, levies, and judgments; and claw back valid liens and payments. A "legal proceeding" means a statutory (or common law) legal process established by the Congress (i.e., the bankruptcy code) or the state legislatures (probates; receiverships; and, in some states, assignments). A business arrangement is an agreement to sell or dispose of assets and pay creditors (bulk sales; workouts; arrangements; and, in some states, assignments). A business arrangement is called an *insolvency process*, as opposed to an *insolvency proceeding*, which is established by law.

The new entrants, which are established by law, are the lien creditors, and they include the bankruptcy trustee, assignee for the benefit of creditors, and equity receivers, who take priority over unsecured creditors, unperfected secured creditors, and tardily filed secured creditors. For example, a bankruptcy trustee enjoys vast statutory rights, including the "strong arm statutes" that dispossess lawful titles to assets held by others [Bankruptcy Code Section 544].

The term *insolvency* can be defined in several ways:

- Insolvency means that the business is unable to pay its liabilities as they accrue. This is called the *equitable definition of insolvency*, and it creates a presumption of insolvency. The debtor might well agree to pay the liabilities through a long term payment program.
- Insolvency means that the liabilities exceed the asset of the business. This is called the *legal definition of insolvency*. This is also called a "balance sheet test," but in practice the assets are valued at their fair market value and not at their "book value."
- Insolvency means that the debtor stopped functioning as an ongoing business; shut the doors; sent the employees home; and faces lawsuits, liens, and levies. This is a commonly understood definition of insolvency. Under these conditions, the debtor's assets might exceed its liabilities; nonetheless, the debtor is sinking into a financial sinkhole. This also includes a debtor facing a large judgment

that might require the debtor to liquidate its assets to pay off the judgment.

- Insolvency means that the debtor liquidates its assets, which makes a pool of funds available for creditors. In some, or many, cases, the liabilities clearly exceed the assets. This could be a pot plan. Expect far more debt than money. Expect pennies on the dollar. Expect a default.
- Insolvency also might mean that the debtor is cash poor but land rich. The debtor lacks the ability to pay its obligations in some lump sum, but could pay the liability when and if an asset is sold. Some cases might hold that a debtor whose assets exceed liabilities is not insolvent, but if the debtor is unable (or unwilling) to pay its current and past liabilities, the debtor is insolvent under the equitable definition. Insolvency means a lack of liquidity, not necessarily an excess of liabilities over debts.

The shortest summary is that the debtor is now dead broke. The debtor cannot pay its creditors. Insolvency instills legal rights and claims in favor of trustee, assignee, receiver, or estate representative, a proceeding that obligates the creditors to timely claims.

The label of insolvency invokes some very serious consequences, as follows:

A. Any transfer by an insolvent of its property for less than fair and equivalent consideration is a fraudulent conveyance, which entitles the creditors of the debtor to recover the assets. The insolvency status of a debtor, in the face of any transfer, is a badge of fraud.

B. Under any commercial loan agreement, being declared insolvent, or insolvent based on a financial statement, constitutes ground to declare the loan due and accelerate all remaining installments. Most major loan agreements compel the debtor to notify the creditor of any change in its financial condition, or grant digital access to its financial records under its noneconomic loan covenants. Many loan agreements pre-define solvency, including inventory receivable and cash ratios, retention of key employees, sales minimums, cash minimums, and payable of ordinary trade debt.

C. Many vendor, supply, government and other major contracts (leases, etc.) require that a party remain in good financial condition (i.e., "solvent"). The fact that the debtor is insolvent might enable the other party to terminate the contract or at least suspend performance.

D. The insolvent nature of the debtor raises concerns about whether the debtor can or will pay payroll, employee taxes due the IRS and the state, franchise taxes (state income taxes), sales tax, and property taxes. Insolvency frightens away key employees, vendors, and management. In a digital world, word of insolvency might go viral.

E. Insolvency is a touchstone in Article 2 of the Uniform Commercial Code (UCC). A vendor might reclaim products sold to an insolvent, assuming timely notice; this can perhaps go back 90 days under UCC Code Section 2702. This is called a claw-back. If a debtor is insolvent, the vendor might demand assurance of payment before proceeding with continuing assets. This is called a demand for adequate assurance under UCC Code Section 2609(1). The fact that a debtor is insolvent might enable the creditor to halt further credit sales (or any sale) based on a reasonable insecurity clause. (See Commercial Code Section 2609(2): "Between merchants the reasonableness of grounds for insecurity and the adequacy of any assurance offered shall be determined according to commercial standards.")

F. Any public entity must report material changes in its financial condition to the SEC, which includes any material adverse change in its financial conditions. Classically, these statements are reflected in an announcement that invokes "substantial doubts about the [debtor's] ability to continue as a going concern" (Public Accounting Oversight Board, AU 341.12). This language—of the "substantial doubts" variety—has entered the American lexicon of public discourse euphemisms next to "retired suddenly to spend more time with family," "suspending operations pending a strategic revamping," or "taking steps to reinvent itself in a new market."

Which Type of Insolvency?

Insolvency cases fall into three easy categories.

Judicially Supervised Proceedings

These include:

- bankruptcies (all Chapters)
- receiverships

- probates and conservatorships (includes trust administration)
- judicially supervised ordered liquidations (depending upon the state assignments, but not all states)
- judicially supervised corporate, LLC, or partnership dissolutions
- restitution claims arising from criminal proceedings or civil forfeiture proceedings
- excess proceeds arising from personal or real property foreclosures deposited into court (real and personal property)
- disputed bulk sales of business that land in court in a dispute over the claim, proceeds, or management of the sale
- some class action cases that offer creditors "pennies on the dollar" for their claims.

These also include mass tort and bankruptcy hybrid funds for asbestos, Dalkon Shield, silicone breast implant, and other large scale tort cases bearing a close similarity to insolvency cases. These cases might offer a fixed pool of money (funds at hand and funds generated over time) to a large group of claimants. While these proceedings are outside the normal parameters of an insolvency (i.e., a failing business), these proceedings bear some of the earmarks of one, which consist of a large group of creditors, a multi-million (or even billion-) dollar creditor class, and a limited distribution. This paradigm describes tobacco and other mass tort trust funds, which the debtor (i.e., the tortfeasor) funds with insurance policies, stock of the revested debtor, or future revenues.

Non-Judicially Supervised Proceedings

These typically include:

- bulk sales and sales of liquor licenses.
- excess proceedings from the foreclosure of personal or real property when the secured creditor has been paid in full, but the foreclosure process generates cash above the secured debt, which enables junior secured claimants to seek payment of their claims. The agent for the foreclosing party cannot sort out the competing claim; the agent (i.e., a stakeholder) will file an interpleader action and deposit funds in court.
- assignments for the benefit of creditors, extensions, compromises, pot plans, or earn-out plans administered by third party creditor associations, such as the National Association of Credit Managers, Credit Managers Associations, trustees, assignees or other creditor bodies, or attorneys for the debtor.

- funds held by insurance companies or third parties to compensate for a mass tort or loss (9-11 Fund, the BP Gulf Settlement, other Kenneth Feinberg funds and similar arrangements). These third party funds are established by the government or private parties, and they offer limited compensation to victims of mass torts or disaster.

Administrative Insolvencies

These include:

- an insurance, bank, credit union, or other regulated entity whose dissolution is overseen by a regulatory entity, such as the FDIC or a state insurance commissioner. (This could cover just about any regulated entity.)
- bond and deposits mandated by federal or state law and made available to claimants. (The most common are bonds for contractors.)
- client security funds for payment of claims asserted by clients who claim embezzlement at the hands of an attorney, crime funds, department of real estate funds, department of industrial relations funds that provide compensation to employees whose employers declined to offer worker's compensation insurance, and similar funds that compensate victims when the third parties lack insurance.

State and federal law offer these funds, whether financed by industry, the state or federal treasury, liquidation of assets, or other sources. The most common is the FDIC. The government oversees these funds, might receive and adjudicate the claims, and distributes a limited recovery to the claimants. The state government department of real estate offers a "real estate recovery fund" to compensate the parties who have been swindled by a real estate broker (or agent). All states have a state bar client security fund that compensates clients who have suffered financial losses arising from attorneys misappropriating or embezzling funds.

Regulated entities (i.e., banks, thrifts, credit unions, insurance companies, stock brokers, among many others) when insolvent come under the jurisdiction of the regulatory entity who might liquidate the regulated entity and pay creditors—or move for the appointment of a receiver who would undertake the same function.

The absolute imperative is that the claimants must timely file and document their claims with the claims administrator and moreover be very watchful for correspondence, including a claim objection, originating from the claim administrator.

These proceedings might be judicial, non-judicial, or administrative, but all bear earmarks of insolvency. These proceedings—no matter their origin or title—marshal, recover, and liquidate the assets of a failed business. The administrative, secured, and priority claimants are paid first, and the balance is paid pro rata to the claimants. Depending upon the fund, the state, and the proceedings, the funds might offer a maximum amount per claimant, no matter the amount of the loss.

2

Assets Grow Feet

Insolvency puts at risk the assets of the insolvent company, which includes the customer list, proprietary information, intellectual property, hard assets, inventory, mailing list, key vendor data, and the digital "rolodex." Any of these might walk out the back door when no one is watching.

Customer Data and Intellectual Property

Presume that insiders, key sales personnel, clerks, or others have illicitly copied and taken the customer list and all proprietary data. In a digital world, we are talking about scraping the company servers of every secret and placing the data on a thumb drive or downloading it to someone's smartphone. Aside from sales information, expect that the stolen information includes all proprietary data, such as market pricing, cost and sale information, formulas, key distributor agreements, and anything else necessary to reconstitute the business in another corporate shell.

Pre-digital customer lists consisted of round rolodex files maintained on employee desks. Each card in the rolodex listed a customer and key personal details. When an employee was about to leave, management would hold onto the rolodex, the physical repository of data. Some employees would manage to grab the company rolodex on their way out the door. (Those of you from the digital generations have probably never seen a rolodex, or, for that matter, a ten key punch, a manual or electric typewriter, or perhaps even an analog wrist watch, but the rolodex was the company's intellectual property treasure trove.)

Today, expect that insiders will steal key proprietary software, either by removing it completely or by making a copy. In businesses that offer IT solutions as their products, the software (and its many incarnations) will exit the back door by 5:00 p.m., or sooner, when the owners announce the end of the business.

If the debtor is a manufacturer, the key assets are tools and dies (and computer programs to run these million dollar machines), custom made manufacturing equipment (and related programs), finished goods attached to a pending sale, work in progress that is very close to completion, and, of course, valuable "raw goods," molds, and additional software that runs the manufacturing process. Osama bin Laden was easier to find than these company assets after closure. Inventory and insurance records likewise disappear, which impedes the recovery of equipment, inventory, and related software. Anything of value might flee.

On the eve of a financial collapse, insiders will transfer the "company jewels" to their new entity, but leave in place hard assets, such as returned or shopworn inventory and other odds and ends. With the trademark in tow, the rest of the intellectual property (IP) bric-a-brac follows out the back door. Check with the United States Patent and Trademark office under the tab of assignments. Don't be surprised to find that the insiders have transferred to their new entity the trademark on the same date they executed an assignment for the benefit of creditors. Advised by their sharpie attorneys, insiders execute a five year, non-interest bearing, unsecured term note for the fair value of the trademark at some nominal price.

How do the insiders get away with the brazen yet entertaining act? Answer: the trademark was attached to a failing business. Ergo, the trademark was valueless. The domain name and email address always follow the trademark. Hard (trademarks, patents, copyrights, etc.) and soft (domain names, telephone and fax numbers, etc.) IP exits the back door and alights into the trunks of the insiders' get-away vehicles.

Transferred Sales Contracts and Purchase Orders

On the eve of the insolvency, the debtor continues to sell or provide services. Standard credit terms are 30 days net. Fixing the drop dead date with near military planning, insiders will often approach the customer with an offer: if the customer pays early (before the doomsday date), the debtor will offer the customer a 20% to 50% discount. Rest assured, nearly all customers jump at the chance. Checks are payable to the debtor, but they are deposited in personal accounts or cashed at the customer's bank. Other times, the checks are deposited into the company bank account, but the proceeds disbursed to pay those obligations are guaranteed by the insiders. Paying off debt subject to a personal guaranty frees the creditors from personal lawsuits and enhances the insider's net worth by debt relief. In more clever cases, the checks are physically held by the insiders, but deposited in their own bank accounts, or in a new bank account, or in a bank account for a successor bearing almost the same name or initials, after the assignment or bankruptcy. This sounds like brazen theft. Forget sounding like anything— this is brazen theft. To avoid detection, the insiders destroy, alter, or make a mess of the financial records to make unwinding this corporate larceny cost prohibitive.

The Secret Cache of Money: Refunds and Forced Overpayments

Insurance Refunds, Earned Premiums, and Rebates

Insolvency leads to a shut down of the company. In the process of liquidation, various "legacy assets" become liquid and generate a cash pay off. Here are a few examples of money coming out of the woodwork. Some of the repositories of funds are known to only a few insiders, which raises the risk of insider theft of assets that are hard to identify, whose loss is only discovered by a later audit (assuming that an audit is even performed).

Eureka #1.   The premiums on workers' compensation are based on the number of employees and the claims history of a company. An unreported reduction in gross salary (fewer employees) or good accident records earn the insured a refund.

Eureka #2.   Cancelling early a prepaid policy, such as liability insurance or a health care policy, gets the insured a refund.

Eureka #3.   The Affordable Care Act demands that insurance companies spend the premiums on health care due the insured and not management salaries and overhead. Insurance companies paid millions in refunds to their insured.

Deposits from Utilities, Leases, and Vendors, and Collateral Securing Credit Instruments (Such as Letters of Credit)

This is another list of hard to detect reservoirs of money that are only known to a select few in the company. Given their low profile, these assets can walk out the door without being missed until a later investigation.

These include refunds that exist on a nearly subliminal basis and only come to fruition when the company ceases to operate. For example, if a tenant vacates an apartment and leaves the place "broom clean" and the rent is current, the landlord must refund the cleaning and security deposit. Midlevel and senior management know where the "bodies" are buried and are quick to reach these barely visible funds. This is not to say that everyone in a failing organization is a petty thief, but when a company fails, theft and vandalism metastasize given the "means and opportunity" and lack of oversight. (Toss in a touch of vengeance at being shown the door.)

For instance, utilities demand two months' deposit for utility service. Landlords demand the first and last month. Certain vendors demand deposits, particularly when the vendor has a lock on the product. Banks demand collateral in hand before issuing a letter of credit, third party debt instruments, or even a company credit card. Collateral might consist of cash on hand, certificate of deposit, stock, viable note secured by a deed of trust, securities, bonds, or anything else of value. When and if the liability on the debt instrument is paid, or the debt instrument is discharged, leaving no contingent liability, the bank will return the collateral, which might be good money. Remember, a bank will generally not issue a $1,000,000.00 letter of credit unless the bank has $1,000,000.00 plus in collateral at hand. Real money.

These are deposits, retainers, security, and collateral that might become liquid if the underlying debt is paid. This is pure cash and on hand and generally known to very few people in the company. Let's reframe the drama. When a company fails, the company becomes a collection of assets that is subject to liquidation and distribution to creditors. Whether a formal bankruptcy, assignment, receivership, bulk sale, workout, or even a probate, a gaggle of creditors are chasing down fewer dollars. While insolvency professionals might boast about 100% solvent recovery for creditors, the usual experience is that creditors receive pennies on the dollar or sometimes slightly more. Insiders, from the president of the company through middle management and the lowliest clerk or hourly employee, see an opportunity to grab valuable assets.

In a digital world with social media and other "connectivity," the most valuable assets are often the intellectual property, which might be trade secrets, computer programs, customer lists, scientific and technical formulas, or product designs. Consider these assets the company's "crown jewels." Insiders know that they can replicate the business in a new shell with this IP as the sparkling nucleus.

Follow the Guideposts to All Proceedings

Presume some slight overlap of rules—depending upon the jurisdiction for each of these insolvency proceedings—but here are the major touchstones for each insolvency, no matter the flavor. In confronting any proceedings, these are the mandatory steps that you need to take in virtually every case.

When Is the Due Date to File the Proof of Claim?

The humorist Douglas Adams was fond of saying, "I love deadlines. I love the whooshing sound they make as they fly by." But the law more often follows Benjamin Franklin's stern admonition: "You may delay, but time will not." Time goes in only one direction. Divining the due date for the filing of the claim is a stop-what-you-are-doing moment.

No matter the flavor of the insolvency, nearly every case requires the creditor to file the claim on time and with the right person. The date to file might appear in the first notice that you receive, or perhaps appear online, or even require research. The most common error is not filing on time. In nearly all cases, the date is a date certain, which means that any late filings are potentially kaput unless the estate is solvent (particularly under bankruptcy). To paraphrase Émile Zola, deadlines are often the terrible anvil on which a legal result is forged (*Anwar v. Johnson*, 720 F.3d 1183, 1184 (9th Cir. 2013)).

Calendar the date, but instead of waiting until the last moment, running smack into a mini disaster that can become a mega disaster, just file the proof of claim when the notice of the insolvency hits your desk. Delay is the enemy. File now and file correctly. Waiting for the last moment invites disaster.

Confirm and triple confirm the address where the claims are to be sent. Check and double check the zip code, department, suite or floor—and the actual name of the court, agency (who would receive claims), or third party claim administrator. Sending the claim without these details can slow or impede the delivery and cause a fatal delay. A botched zip code is a botched claim. Don't leave the task to an assistant or junior associate. Do it yourself.

Even if the claim is incomplete, file now—you can amend the claim later and add information. If you do wind up late, file the claim anyway. Anecdotal evidence (fancy words for by guess and by golly) is that creditors bungle filings in every case. If an estate is solvent, a late claim might be paid. Depending upon the particular insolvency, you can seek relief from a late filing. If notice to file the claim was inadequate, incomplete, or otherwise bungled, the court might allow a late filed claim. As we explain later, informal notice of the proceeding is notice of all dates, including the bar date to file a claim. Do not wait until formal notice is received. This would be a major error.

What to File

In many judicial proceedings, you are required to use the form mandated by the court or third party claim administrator, along with the place, date, and method of filing. These forms are online, or offered by the claim administrator. The form identifies the case and case number; requires that you identify the claimant, the amount, the interest, and security; and asks for back up documentation and how to reach you. Again, endeavor to use the form provided to you. In a non judicial insolvency, the assignee or liquidator might demand that you use their form. Don't blow that off. Attach everything in support of the claim, including all documents that you would offer into evidence in a trial. Make sure that the claim is current with interest calculated to the date of filing, along with all allowable court costs and attorney's fees. Failure to attach documentation might lead to a claim objection. If the claim is secured, attach every scratch of paper that would support the claim and, more importantly, the security interest. Absent clear and comprehensive documentation, the trustee might assert that your claim is unsecured because you did not attach the supporting documentation. This is an expensive and possibly fatal error.

However, if the debt arises from a consumer transaction, the proof of claim is potentially subject to the Fair Debt Collection Practices Act. The federal and state FDCPA requires enormous rigor in the filing of a proof of claim. Errors here dig the graves of consumer collection attorneys. The rules are simple. Be wary of time barred claims that violate the FDCPA (depending upon the circuit). Insure that the claim is very accurate, which includes the accrued interest, rate of interest, and whether the claim is secured. Avoid attaching documents that reveal a social security number. Insure that the precise name of the creditor is correct. Always ask for a file stamped and confirmed copy to insure that the claim got there.

Claims arising from civil or criminal restitution proceedings are controlled by statutes that necessitate careful compliance. Depending upon the type of the forfeiture proceeding, the claimant might have to demonstrate a property "interest" in the forfeited property seized by the government. The victims of Ponzi schemes endeavor to trace their money, when possible, to the bank accounts seized by the government. Restitution proceedings are very time sensitive and again, more importantly, require detailed supporting documentation. File with the court, if required, and file with the agency (or agencies). In some cases, the claimant might have to file with the court, the agency, the U.S. Attorney for the district, the Department of Justice, or others. In restitution matters, the devil is in the details. Read the filing instructions. Please note that the government posts forfeiture proceedings online. You can ask for notice of these proceedings. If the claim is secured, attach the documents that prove up the security interest. If the security is valueless, or the claim is only partially secured, make that clear. Attach the filed or recorded deed of trust, UCC, mortgage, or other security device. This is an imperative.

If the claim arose during the insolvency proceeding (bankruptcy, particularly a Chapter 11), the creditor might be entitled to administrative status. As for any claim, you must attach supporting documentation that is very clear, easy to understand, and complete. Claims agents are not certified public accountants and lack the time to do your math homework. Always attach a summary sheet that is supported by the invoices, contracts, and final accounting.

If this is a bankruptcy, you need to file a motion to compel payment and allow your administrative claim, in addition to filing a proof of claim. Remember, you are not alone. The bankruptcy might be administratively insolvent if the administrative creditors exceed the funds on hand. More than one bankruptcy has paid administrative creditors pennies on the dollar. Moreover, filing an administrative claim invokes different filing protocols, such as due dates, the form of the proof claim, the identities of the many folks who are entitled to receive the proof of claim and specific supporting paperwork. The courts issue these orders, which you should follow to a T. Watch for special court orders in mega cases that spell out the procedures for the filing of administrative claims, which might include a bar date for filing, the place of filing, a specific form of claim, requirements for specific documentation, identification and specification of the parties or attorneys who are entitled to receive copies of the notice, or a requirement to respond to any claim inquiry or objection. These rules are inflexible and require complete compliance.

If the debtor has your property (as opposed to a debt), the filing of the proof of claim has to communicate that you want the property back. If you are not careful, the administrator might claim that, by virtue of the money demand, you are taking the position that you have sold the personal property to the debtor, who is therefore the owner thereof; thus, you are only owed damages by virtue of nonpayment of the sale price. If the Chapter 11 offers creditors 5% on the dollar, your proof of claim might convert a claim for property that has great value to a small proof claim worth 5% on the dollar for the hardware.

Administrative proceedings require the use of forms mandated by claim administrator. These proceedings include claims filed before the State Insurance Commission, the FDIC, and other federal and state agencies. These forms mandate that the claimant specify the amount due, the supporting documentation, proof of the debt and proof of any security, and any supporting documentation.

If you are dealing with a bulk sale, business sale, sale of a liquor license, or other non judicial sale, you might be able to file a letter claim supported by the underlying invoices, statements, and other proof of the debt. You can fax letter claims—and even sometimes email them—but it is always best, when possible, to get them there via "paper" overnight. To avoid an unnecessary objection, attach all supporting documentation, which might include invoices, statements, proof of delivery, and copies of any notes or written promises to pay. Also, include the principal balance due, the accrued interest, the attorney's fees and court costs, and accruing interest to the date of payments. The escrow holder declines to do your math.

If a claim is entitled to priority by statute or otherwise (wages, taxes, administrative claims, or secured claims), the claimant bears the affirmative burden to state the requirements for the priority in the proof of claim. The claimant must prove up the priority status in the claim by attaching documentation and reciting the body of law that supports the priority status.

How to Get the Form to the Claim Administrator

If you are working with a bankruptcy proceeding, you can electronically file the proof of claim. If you are not ECF qualified, file the proof of claim via paper. Always transmit the proof of claim through a recognized overnight service, such as Fed Ex, DHL, UPS, or other courier service. Mail is very slow. Return receipt mail is glacial—and fatal if the due date is approaching. Bankruptcy, probate, conservatorship, and other form proceedings require that you use their forms. Secure and maintain proof of delivery. More than one pundit calls due dates "drop dead dates," with good reason.

Who Gets the Claim?

Mega debtors appoint a commercial claims agent to receive, deem filed with the court, and archive the proofs of claims. In these monster cases, you will find fairly early a court order on the docket designating a claims agent. Read their filings instructions, which might be different from those for filing with the court. Claims agents offer indexing of claims, which enables you to quickly confirm that your claim got filed, the date of filing, and the status of the claim.

Filing a claim is a serious process. You must read the instructions. In filing an administrative claim in a Chapter 11, depending upon the court order (if any), the creditor has to serve the debtor, debtor's counsel, committee attorney, committee chair, U.S. Trustee, and claims administrator, among others. In some cases, notice is due by noon, Eastern Standard Time, on some specific date. Always, without fail, check the docket to see if the court has already entered an order that mandates a special procedure for filing and payment of administrative claims. If it has, filing a proof of claim for an administrative claim is ineffective. The creditor must file a motion with the court to have the administrative claim paid. If the case is a Chapter 11, the plan process might impose very tight requirements to file and serve an administrative claim. The procedures might be part of a separate proceeding, or incorporated into the disclosure statement or the plan itself. This search of the claim process is very arduous, but an absolute necessity.

In a probate proceeding, filing a claim in probate requires filing the claim with the court, with the estate representative, and with the attorney for the representative. Filing claims in a probate is hyper time sensitive. Delay is deadly.

In a criminal or civil restitution proceeding, whether state or federal, the claimant must file the claim with the court, the agency that might have possession of the property, and the prosecutor, among others required by a court order or local rules.

Claim filing instructions might appear in the claim notice, but for many insolvencies, you have to read the statute or agency rules. Failure to serve the specified designees might doom your claim. Read the claim manual for each proceeding.

Remain Vigilant

Chapter 11 and 13 bankruptcies are frequently dismissed with limited notice. If the case is dismissed before the debtor files a complete list of creditors, many creditors, aware of the bankruptcy, might not get notice of the dismissal by mail, although the dismissal will appear on the court's docket. Escrow holders, liquidators, and attorneys might resign from an insolvency case or proceeding in which the creditor might have notice. Troubled escrows might compel an escrow holder to resign and be slow in informing the creditors of the change of escrow holder. You might or might not learn about the next filings or find out about the successor insolvency administrator until the bar date has come and gone.

In any case, always file a request for special notice that will insure notice of all proceedings, including the hearing that might lead to the dismissal of the bankruptcy. If granted, expect new and replacement filings by the debtor. These debtors are called serial files. Serial filing is a fact of life and requires attention to detail (particularly the new case number). Filing a request for special notice enables a creditor to better follow a proceeding and reduce the risk of missing the dismissal; the request for special notice provides many warnings of a potential and maybe onrushing dismissal.

Be Accurate and Careful

Most insolvencies are judicially supervised and subject to their own bodies of laws, such as bankruptcy. Claims filed with a federal entity are subject to federal anti-fraud criminal statutes. Filing a false proof of claim is a crime. Proofs of claims are filed under penalty of perjury. Endeavor to accurately, correctly, and truthfully complete the form. Attach all supporting documents. Make sure that you have, and can preserve, proof for each claim, should the matter be litigated. If a claim is wrong, file an amended claim as soon as possible. Diligence rides shotgun in filing a proof of claim.

Does an Administrator, Debtor, or Third Party Have the Right to Dispute the Claim?

Consider the claim a well-pled civil complaint that is filed in a court. The debtor, other creditors, secured creditors, or administrator has the right to object to your claim. This means that your claim is now "at issue," which requires you to respond to the claim objection on a very *timely* basis. In most, but not all cases, parties resolve their claim objections either upon a letter that highlights some defect, or the filing of the objection. Always remember that the trustee or debtor's attorney has carefully calendared a response. Expect a default to be automatically filed. All extensions should be filed with the court. In other cases, the objecting party pursues a strategy of objecting to the proofs of claims under the belief that the claimants will decline to respond given the low dollar amount involved or the rigor of hiring local and sometimes expensive counsel. In some Chapter 11s, the debtors will object to every claim based on "inadequate documentation" and score an 80% or better knockout rate.

Keep Current: Request for Special Notice and Post Office Box

Bankruptcy and probate proceedings allow a creditor to receive mailed (and electronic, for bankruptcy) notice of all proceedings in the court. Requesting special notice is paramount to keep everyone informed, which is crucial in these cases. Better yet, you can demand that the client receive direct notice to insure that the client receives up to date information. A request for special notice gives the creditor a ring side seat for all proceedings.

Any formal or informal insolvency proceeding might take years to complete. Three to five years is not unusual. Some cases continue for 60 or more months. This is common in administrative liquidations of banks, credit unions, and insurance companies. Big Chapter 11s frequently take 60-plus months from the filing to the plan confirmation. You might want to rent a local post office box as your permanent address for the receipt of any notice—including, most importantly, any claim objection—and of course, any distribution. Bankruptcy and third party administrators assume that you will keep everyone apprised of your address. Given the nature of large law firms, keeping everyone notified—including trustees, administrators, and liquidators—of your changes of address can be problematic. Avert this mail crisis; use a permanent post office box. Little details become big nightmares if the mail is misdirected or sidetracked based on a faulty address.

Selling the Claim

Expect in large Chapter 11 cases an offer from a hedge fund (or professional claims buyer) to buy your proof of claim. Prices range from 10 to 90 cents on the dollar. For some creditors, this is an attractive option. One downside is that the creditor indemnifies the buyer in the event of claim litigation and warrants the claim is valid and subsisting. Another is that the rule of thumb is that the claim buyer is paying about 50% of the real value of the claim. Claim buying reduces the risk of an uncertain recovery; on the other hand,

Chapter 11s, particularly very large cases, have a good track record that enable the creditor to predict the outcome.

In mega bankruptcy cases, expect multiple offers (perhaps a dozen) from claims buyers, whose prices might rise and fall based on the state of the case. These prices are competitive. Claims buyers employ staffs of sophisticated and experienced bankruptcy attorneys, financial analysts, and accountants who do a first rate job of predicting the outcome of the case. Their offers represent a discount based on their projection of the final distribution.

Automatic Stay or Immunity from Enforcement or Futile Enforcement

Upon the filing of a bankruptcy, the court enters (by law) an automatic stay that stops all collection or enforcement against the debtor or the debtor's assets. However, the creditor is free to prosecute litigation on the personal guaranty against third party guarantors. Consider a bankruptcy stay immunity from collection or enforcement.

On the other hand, if there is a bona fide assignment for the benefit of the creditors, a suit against the debtor is futile because the debtor assigned its assets to the assignee. Collection or enforcement against the assets of the debtor is futile. Call this an empty cupboard moment.

Receiverships are a little different. While a receivership might not (depends on the state and court order) stop or preclude a lawsuit against the debtor whose assets are subject to the receivership, the assets are in the custody and control of the court and immune from any enforcement. Trying to reach assets subject to a receivership might subject the creditor to contempt of court.

Stay Alert: More Details to Watch For

This section lists the evils that fled from Pandora's box.

You Have to Pay a Fee to File a Proof of Claim

In some probate proceedings, the court requires a filing fee. This is a shocker because most attorneys believe that filing a proof of claim is free. Not so. Check with the court's website.

The court might not accept a business check but only a cashier's check or post office money order. This is not the law in bankruptcy court, but sometimes fees are demanded in probate courts. This is inexplicable and inherently unfair. If the fee is not attached to the proof of claim, and the claim is filed on the last day but rejected, re-filing the claim with the check at hand will have to be done late—which might be fatal. Always double check local rules in the filing of any claim or other proceedings. Local rules will humble the greatest. A common refrain in bankruptcy court is "I did not check the local rules . . ."

Vote for Me or You Get Nothing

Some Chapter 11 plans require that you affirmatively vote for the plan, or you will not get paid under the timely filed proof of claim. Read the plan and disclosure statement very carefully. Whether this term is fair or unfair is not the point. The point is that the creditor, no matter the amount, is required to read the disclosure statement and the plan or reorganization to insure payment of a claim. This burden raises issues of unfairness if the creditor's claim is modest in amount, the disclosure statement and plan are particularly voluminous, and the requirement to vote for the plan is buried somewhere.

A Taxpayer Identification Number Is Required

The Chapter 11 plan requires that you file your consent timely and include the taxpayer identification number (TIN) or social security number (SSN). Another hurdle to getting paid. This is a little silly because the debtor, before the case, was paying its creditors without requiring a TIN.

Global Releases on the Backs of Checks

If your case is an out of court insolvency, read the back of the check extremely carefully. Rest assured that the back of the check bears the following inscription: "Cashing, endorsing or retaining this check constitutes full and final payment of the claim of this creditor and discharges the liability of everyone and anyone who has guaranteed this obligation or jointly liable, secondarily liable, or liable as co-maker, accommodation party, surety, or guarantor and discharges any security interest, mortgage, interest or lien." Be wary in any large financial transaction; the guaranty of the corporate parent of the subsidiary's debt is exonerated (i.e., expired—stone cold and very dead) if the subsidiary pays off more than 50% of the guaranteed debt, including any debt owed to the corporate parent. To avoid this check being cycled through the client's "lock box," which provides for an instantaneous deposit, the claim form or letter should clearly direct the claims administrator to pay you (i.e., the attorney) by forwarding a paper check to your offices.

Be further alert in any formal or informal proceeding, that the insiders, who guaranteed your debt and other creditors', frequently offer the estate administrator a significant sum of money in exchange for a global release of all guaranties held by creditors who individually decline to consent. A court might confirm a Chapter 11 that discharges the claims of creditors against third party guarantors, and this is more likely if the guarantor put money in the case. In a non bankruptcy setting, the guarantor would make the offer, which is solicited among the creditors, who are required to "sign-off" as a inducement for the guarantor to make this contribution.

Where Are You on the Pecking Order?

Chapter 11 plans can create an waterfall of payments by classifying creditors. Be alert that the purpose of this classification to avoid payment completely. In following the case, and in filing the proof of claim, be alert for plan treatment. Consider a chapter plan and disclosure statement a minefield that might cause damage based on any misstep.

Claims That Echo

A proof claim in a bankruptcy is a complaint of sorts. Complaints represent an admissible expression of the claimant's factual and legal claims. In ensuing, or even parallel proceedings, third parties can introduce the claim into evidence. In other proceedings, the claim might estop the claimant from litigating an amount that is different (usually greater) than the proof of claim. The claim might estop the claimant from asserting security if omitted from the claim. If the claim is paid, allowed, or "adjudicated," the claim might even support collateral estoppel or judicial estoppel in another proceeding. The punch line is that the claimant should be very careful with any statement or claim made in the proof of claim because those statements or claims might find their way into other proceedings. This is called the law of unintended consequences.

Case law embraces the expression "blowing hot and cold." Given digital access to federal filings through PACER and growing parallel access in the state courts, any filing is now accessible, particularly a claim filed in a bankruptcy case.

A Confirmed Plan Adjudicates Collateral Claims and Rights

What does this mean? A confirmed plan is a judgment of the federal court and therefore bears all the characteristics of both collateral estoppel and res judicata. This is another Read the Plan and Disclosure Statement moment (i.e., read the manual). Disclosure statements and proposed plans of reorganization can span, together, 750 pages. Somewhere in there is one of those large or small stink bombs that might foreclose third party litigation.

Consider a prime example. The debtor filed Chapter 11. The debtor is a general partnership in which the general partners are independently liable for the debts. The debtor gets a plan confirmed that discharges the liability of the individual partners. The confirmed plan bars creditors from suing the partners in state court.

Expect the plan to extinguish the guaranties owed by the insiders to the creditors, eliminate surety and indemnities obligation owed by insiders and non debtor related entities, and exonerate the bond liability of third parties that are due creditors, consumers, and claimants.

Let's step back here. Insolvency offers a fund of money to creditors. A creditor must file a proof of claim to assert an interest in the funds. The creditor must comply with the claim filing rules and read everything filed in the case. If it's a Chapter 11, the plan is the "playbook" that offers the creditor some type of recovery, big or small (and sometimes really small). The task befalling the creditor is navigating the claim process and avoiding "unforced" errors.

The next chapter shows how to preserve the creditor's right to pursue a guarantor. In most major transactions, the creditor has secured a personal guaranty that becomes very important because the insolvency might have generated only pennies on the dollar.

When the insolvency door closes, the door to the guarantor opens.

Beware Exoneration of the Guarantor

Under general surety law, the creditor is obligated to exercise diligence in pursuing all rights and remedies in collecting the debt from the debtor. Diligence means chasing down the debtor with all due speed and thoroughness. In the land of litigation against guarantors, and in the face of diligence borne by the creditor as a pre-requisite against recovering against the guarantor, nice guys finish last.

This is the duty of diligence frame of California Civil Code Section 2845:

> A surety may require the creditor . . . to proceed against the principal, or to pursue any other remedy in the creditor's power which the surety cannot pursue, and which would lighten the surety's burden; and if the creditor neglects to do so, the surety is exonerated to the extent to which the surety is thereby prejudiced.

To define our terms: A guarantor is another person who promises to pay the debt of the debtor. A guaranty must be in writing and signed by the guarantor. The guaranty is an offer to pay the debt of the debtor. Absent terms in the contract, the creditor accepts the the offer when the creditor extends credit to the debtor. The credit might consist of the sale of goods or rendition of services on a credit basis. The credit might consist of a loan of money or other financial accommodation to the the debtor or a third person. In a business proposition, the creditor demands, and receives, a guaranty because the creditor perceives that the debtor might not pay the obligation when due. Inevitably, the creditor will demand a personal guaranty from the principal of the debtor. When the principal of the debtor guaranties the debt of the debtor, the principal will cause the debtor to pay the debts owed to creditor holding a guaranteed debt in order to eliminate the guarantor's contingent liability.

Most commercial guaranties used by banks, sophisticated vendors, landlords, and leasing companies, among others, demand waiver of due diligence and all related obligations. In fact, these waivers are routine; they are part and parcel of commonly used forms in the legal community. Virtually every template for a personal guaranty provides for this waiver, along with others. These waivers are never implied; they must be clearly stated. Three pages of waivers is about average. Without a citation of extensive case law, here are the three rules of drafting that apply to guaranties:

1. All ambiguities are construed against the drafter (who is the creditor in nearly all cases).
2. All ambiguities are construed against the drafter (the creditor) of a pre-printed form.
3. Waivers in personal guaranties are never presumed, and a court will not mine (i.e., as one mines for gold) a personal guaranty to reconstruct a presumed waiver. (The court is not going to excavate a waiver out of some vaguely written language.)

Suffice to say, and without reference to pages of citations, judges routinely let guarantors off the hook because the waivers are missing, poorly drafted, or ambiguous. Without a citation to any authority, other than unreliable, unverifiable, anecdotal evidence, judges will *routinely* topple personal guaranties because they dislike imposing liability for someone else's debt. Also, a personal guaranty must be in writing under the statute of frauds and signed by the guarantor.

Here is a long list of unforced errors in insolvency proceedings that might exonerate the guaranty of liability under the guaranty and leave the creditor "high and dry":

1. Failure to timely file a proof of claim in the debtor's bankruptcy or other insolvency case.
2. Failure to perfect the security interest by filing, or recording, a timely UCC (financing statement), which renders the security interest unperfected and voidable in a bankruptcy, assignment for the benefit of creditors, or receiver in equity, or which renders it subject to subordination by a senior perfected creditor. This also includes the failure to timely renew the financing statement by filing a continuation statement. Another common error is the failure to perfect a security interest in leasehold improvement and trade fixtures that require recording the UCC with the county recorder. Perfecting a security interest in a copyright requires the filing with the U.S. Copyright Office. Perfecting a security interest in a patent requires a filing with the secretary of state, but maybe filing with the United States Patent and Trademark Office (USPTO). Maybe. Perfection of agricultural lien might require recording the UCC. This includes a security interest in aquatic species (fish). The perfecting of a security interest is serious endeavor. Anticipating

down the road a potential insolvency, a cautious business attorney should engage specialized counsel, versed in secured transactions, to properly perfect the security interest. If the collateral is intellectual property, and particularly a copyright, counsel should likewise engage an IP attorney to perfect the security, as required, through the U.S. Copyright Office, and USPTO for patents and/or trademarks. Perfection of a security interest is very technical and very unforgiving. Botching security is a common error of the creditor, which lets the guarantor off the hook completely.

3. Failure to include the total unpaid balance, which consists of principal, interest, costs, and attorneys' fees, and interest to date. This might sound like a tiny misstep, but if the creditor botches the basic demand, the guarantor is off the hook.

4. Failure to enforce the security interest against assets, or their proceeds, in the hands of the trustee, debtor, or assignee. This error arises when the trustee, debtor, or assignee comes into assets subject to a security interest or reclamation claim. Unfortunately, the trustee, debtor, or assignee liquidates these assets that might be subject to other claims or even expended.

5. Failure to respond to adversary complaints, contested matters, sale applications, motions to surcharge collateral (Bankruptcy Code Section 506(c)), that might alter, change, or prejudice the rights of the secured creditor. These proceedings might damage, shrink, or destroy the security interest and render the creditor unsecured. Failure to assert a priority claim under 11 U.S.C. § 503: US Code—Section 503 Bankruptcy Code 503(b)(9) for goods sold and delivered within 20 days prior to the filing date. This includes the failure to file a motion to compel payment of administrative claim or to adhere to procedure that would provide for payment of these claims. This is a common error. Goods sold within 20 days of a bankruptcy proceeding are entitled to priority status and a greater likelihood of payment.

6. Failure to prosecute reclamation right in any proceeding under Commercial Code Section 2702 (sales to an insolvent) or under Bankruptcy Code Section 546. This is another big deal. Recapturing the goods when sold to an insolvent is an act of clear diligence. Letting the goods "go down the drain" would damage the creditor's chance to recover based on the claimed goods.

7. Failure to suspend performance and mitigate the claim if the debtor is insolvent under Commercial Code Section 2609 (e.g., stop

shipping product). This remedy enables the creditor to minimize and reduce the risk of loss. Selling to a known insolvent might discharge the guarantor.

8. Failure to stop, turn around, or recover product in transit under Commercial Code 2703(a)-(f). The remedy enables a creditor to recover, retrieve or capture goods in transit and therefore mitigate the loss.

9. Failure to object to senior claims that are inflated, bogus, or fraudulent, which, if allowed, would deplete the estate and diminish the recovery due the creditor. This is a touch tricky. Insolvencies are fill of "gold diggers" who file false and inflated claims that deplete the estate. Objecting to these bogus claims will increase the balance due the creditor because the dollars that might have gone to the charlatans are now cycled downward for payment due the creditors.

10. Failure to timely file suit and obtain a pre-judgment writ of attachment that might encumber the assets of the debtor and, depending upon timing, survive any later challenge. The short version: You snooze, You lose. If the debtor is in default, file suit and attach. If the debtor defaulted in favor of one creditor, chances are the debtor owes everyone up and down the street, and they might be more ambitious and more likely to tie up the assets. This is a case of the early bird gets and worm.

11. Failure, post judgment, to impose liens by way of a recorded abstract of judgment, filed personal property lien, or issued and served debtor's examination order that would impose a potentially unavoidable lien on the assets. This includes the failure to properly name or identify the correct liable party and insure that the judgment debtor is the entity who holds and owns the debtor's apparent property. The failure to record basic liens is the fastest way to let the guarantor off the hook. These liens might generate full payment. The failure to file the liens might generate full payment for the junior or other competing creditors.

12. Failure to recognize and perfect a security interest buried in a lease, credit application, invoice, or "terms and conditions" that converts an unsecured creditor into a secured creditor. Many commercial personal property leases incorporate broad security interest in all assets. The failure to assert and perfect the liens might exonerate the guarantor.

13. Failure to promptly recover collateral subject to a security interest and provide for timely sale. In the event of a catastrophic default, the debtor might refuse to turn over the collateral that secures a debt. The creditor must exercise diligence to recover the collateral, which might disappear or suffer vandalism, damage, destruction, or fire. Should the collateral "take flight" or otherwise be unavailable for any reason, the guarantor will claim exoneration based on the creditor's lack of diligence.

14. Proceeding with a non judicial foreclosure of real property, but attempting to impose liability under the personal guarantor in which the guarantor's subrogation rights are effectively eviscerated without seeking, at the outset, a clear and unequivocal waiver (depending upon the taste).

15. Failure to immediately file an action (or other motion) in bankruptcy court if the debtor is wrongfully converting the debtor's cash collateral, which effectively renders the creditor "unsecured," and therefore exposes the personal guarantor. See Bankruptcy Code Section 363(e). More than once, a debtor has liquidated cash collateral or disposed of goods subject to reclamation. The creditor might be granted an administrative claim, but the estate might be administratively insolvent, which means that administrative claims are paid pennies on the dollar or nothing at all.

This list is illustrative and not exhaustive.

The attorney for the guarantor will plead "failure to exhaust remedies" as an affirmative defense, which, if proven, supports exoneration of the guarantor. Any of these errors might get the guarantor off the hook for a million dollar liability.

The next chapter discusses the basic rules of personal property security. Personal property security gives the creditor the legal right to seize, voluntarily or through legal process, personal property. Based on the security interest, the creditor can sell the personal property and apply the proceeds to payment of the debtor.

5

A Primer for UCC Priorities

What Is a Security Interest?

Let's do the ABCs of a security interest. A security interest is a lien on personal property. This security interest is the legal right of the creditor (the "secured party") to take possession (or, better stated, repossession) of the personal property. Upon recovery of the personal property, the secured creditor has the legal right to sell, or liquidate, the personal property and apply the proceeds to the payment of the debt.

The most common form of security is the lien on a car to insure that the owner makes payment to the finance company. Businesses finance their equipment purchases through a leasing company, hard money financier, bank, or long term financing offered by the seller. Long term financing is commonly called "captive financing," which is sometimes offered at attractive rates. Businesses, including attorneys, doctors, dentists, and manufacturers in the garment and fashion business, among others, finance their receivables. Despite the machinations of account receivable financing, which is called factoring, the simple explanation is that the financier lends money on the receivable, or actually buys the receivable at a steep discount.

The law of secured transaction is found in Article 9 of the Uniform Commercial Code, which all states have enacted. Generally, and with very few exceptions, the law of secured transactions is reasonably uniform in all states. Security interest would reach the property in existence and hereinafter acquire property, proceeds, profits, replacements, and accessories.

The two basic steps of all security are, first, that the debtor signs a written security agreement that describes the collateral with some reasonable specificity. This is called the security agreement. "I grant You, Secured Creditor, security in my ABC machine to secure the debt that I owe You. If I do not pay You, You can repossess the machine" would be more than legally sufficient. The next step is to file a financing statement in the offices of the secretary of state where the debtor "resides," which is a fancy term for the place of incorporation. If the security is lease, trade fixture, incorporated in the real property, agricultural products, minerals in the grounds, fish, or other like items, the creditor records the financing statement in the county where the collateral is located. This is called perfecting the security interest. A financing statement has a five year life and must be renewed.

The security interest, if perfected, offers the creditor priority—based on the time of filing—against the rights of other secured creditors. The security interest might take priority over a subsequent bankruptcy trustee, debtor in possession, assignee for the benefit of creditor, equity receiver, or judgment and lien creditor (including federal and state taxes and other governmental liens—family law).

What Happens to a Security Interest in Insolvency?

The Uniform Commercial Code (the law in all states) offers the creditor a seat at the insolvency table and sometimes at the head of the table. The secured creditor might even control the case, or enjoy the highest priority for payment, which might include all pre and post petition attorney's fees, interest, and costs. On the other hand, filing a judicial insolvency proceeding (i.e., a bankruptcy) means that the debtor invites another party (the trustee) to the table who can legally reorder lien priorities and unwind secured liens under the Strong Arm Powers. Call this the insolvency potluck dinner—bring your rights and liabilities to the dinner table and have fun.

If and when consensual liens (the security interest) are subordinated, unwound, or dissolved, the insolvency restores the debtor's newly revived equities to the estate. Dumping a security interest frees up money. Upon liquidation of the recovered equities (unencumbered assets), the estate can pay the debtor's non-dischargeable debts, including domestic support obligations and taxes. Taxes and family law obligations are non-dischargeable (Bankruptcy Code Section 523(a)(1) [most taxes] and (5) [domestic support obligations]). These obligations are also priority obligations in a distribution. (See Bankruptcy Code Sections 507(a)(1)(A)-(B) about family support, 507(a)(8) about taxes, and 507(a)(10) about drunk driving injuries.)

Consider the classic case in which a bankruptcy frees up equity that could pay off the non-dischargeable debts: The debtor owes big time family and child support, which are priority claims and non-dischargeable. Unfortunately, the debtor also ran up a slew of credit card bills. Credit card companies bundle up their "charge-offs" and sell them as large dollar packages to "debt buyers." Debt buyers sue, serve, and take judgment. Upon entry of judgment, the debt buyer records liens. These liens chew up the equity in the debtor's home. If these liens are older than 90 days, the liens survive bankruptcy. If the debtor sells his home, he pays off the old credit card bills, but still faces the non-dischargeable child support and taxes. Facing this risk, the debtor would file bankruptcy for the purpose of unwinding these credit card liens, sell or refinance them, and pay off the child support or the taxes that will probably never go away.

The moral of this tale is that the insolvency administrator (the trustee or assignee) can unwind liens, levies, and transfers that back unencumbered assets to the estate that produce payment to priority and non-dischargeable debts. Stated succinctly, the enemy of my enemy is my friend.

The Pecking Order

Getting to know the "pecking order" is important because moving up or down the pecking order is the difference between getting paid or getting stiffed. The T-Shirt version of priorities says "The Early Bird Gets the UCC Worm."

Here is the starting point: A trustee, an assignee for the benefit of creditors, an equity receiver, or a creditor with execution or attachment levies is a 'lien creditor' (Uniform Commercial Code Section Code Section 9102(a)(52)). The filing of an insolvency creates a lien creditor, who becomes a party to any secured transaction. Below are listed the UCC priorities, which reflect the rights of the lien creditor.

1. A buyer in the ordinary course of business beats out a prior per-fected security interest, even if the buyer has knowledge (UCC Section 9320(a)). What does this mean in English? The lender who floored automobiles, household appliances, electronics, and inven-tory cannot chase down the customers should the retailer default the loan.

2. A bulk sale buyer (or non course of business buyer) for value and without notice beats out the unperfected security interest, without knowledge of the security and before it its perfected (UCC Section 9317(b)). What does this mean in English? The buyer in bulk, which is usually the sale of a business, beats out a secured creditor who failed to file (or record) the financing statement (UCC).

3. A lien creditor beats out a later filed (perfected) security interest. (UCC Section 9317(a)(2)(A): "Security interest or agricultural lien is subordinate to the rights of: (1) a person entitled to priority under Section 9-322; and (2) except as otherwise provided in sub-section (e), *a person that becomes a* lien creditor *before the earlier of the time: (A) the security interest or agricultural lien is perfected*; or . . .") This is a very big deal. The lien creditor beats out the later filed secured interest. This priority is a touch redundant because of other curlicues. Upon the filing of a bankruptcy, the debtor's

property passes to the trustee (or debtor in possession), which means that the debtor no longer has 'rights' that a security interest could encumber (Bankruptcy Code Section 541). The strong arm statute subordinates the later filed liens (Bankruptcy Code Section 544). Filing the lien after the filing of the bankruptcies violates the automatic stay (Bankruptcy Code Section 362(a)(3)-(5) seq.). The later filed liens would be subordinate to an assignee because upon the assignment, the assignee takes title to the assignor's property, which would likewise apply in an equity receivership.

4. The earlier filed perfected security interest beats out the later filed perfected security interest (UCC Section 9322(a)(1)). This is the standard first to file rule. Remember, a debtor does NOT need to sign the UCC. Moreover, many commercial services will electronically file the UCC.

5. A perfected security interest (filed) beats out the unperfected security interest (UCC Section 9322(a)(2)). This rule is the shorthand for the prior common concept that the filing of a deed, mortgage, etc. would beat out the unfiled competing claim.

6. The first unperfected security interest beats another unperfected security interest by order of attachment (UCC Section 9322(a)(3)). Many personal and real property leases, credit applications, sales contractors, and 'terms and conditions' demanded by a vendor incorporate into their boilerplate a blanket security interest. This is a near expectation.

This is a short summary of a complex topic. These rules are very important because a trustee, assignee, or equity receiver, all creatures of insolvency, beat out later filed perfected creditors. Besides equity receivers, trustees in bankruptcy (and debtors in possession) and some assignees can "claw back" a perfected security interest if preferential.

Getting a lien on the assets of the debtor elevates a creditor from unsecured to secured. Assuming that the creditor secured the lien outside the 90-day pre-filing window (and absent other defenses), the creditor enters the proceedings as a secured creditor. Depending upon the "pecking order," the creditor might exit the case with money in hand (perhaps just some money in hand, but something is better than nothing).

Some people think that dogs and cats can anticipate earthquakes. Maybe or maybe not, but a touch of clairvoyance can prompt us to raise the curtain on the dying debtor. What happens when the debtor is going down the drain? Read the next chapter to learn how to hit the brakes before a little loss becomes a big loss and a big loss becomes a disaster.

6

Suspension of Performance and Insolvency Options

This section explains that "where there's smoke, there's fire" and "a stitch in time saves nine." Both expressions are part of the UCC. UCC Code Section 2069 enables a party to suspend performance under a contract when the other party (usually the buyer of goods) is suffering financial palpitations. Life support is never good. Section 2609 provides as follows:

(1) A contract for sale imposes an obligation on each party that the other's expectation of receiving due performance will not be impaired. When reasonable grounds for insecurity arise with respect to the performance of either party, the other may in writing demand adequate assurance of due performance and, until he receives such assurance, may if commercially reasonable suspend any performance for which he has not already received the agreed return.

(2) Between merchants, the reasonableness of grounds for insecurity and the adequacy of any assurance offered shall be determined according to commercial standards.

(3) Acceptance of any improper delivery or payment does not prejudice the aggrieved party's right to demand adequate assurance of future performance.

(4) After receipt of a justified demand, failure to provide within a reasonable time (not exceeding 30 days) such assurance of due performance as is adequate under the circumstances of the particular case is a repudiation of the contract.

What does this mean in English? Well, fire fighters are hailed when they run into burning buildings. Law enforcement is lauded when the officers rush to an active shooter scene. On the other hand, the UCC Code Section 2609 tells the vendor to "get out of dodge" before the debtor goes bankrupt, makes an assignment, or collapses under the weight of foreclosing secured creditors. UCC 2609 enables a seller to mitigate its losses by stopping sales, putting product on credit hold, or freezing production.

In true UCC jargon, Section 2609 enables the seller to suspend sales based on "reasonable grounds for insecurity." Upon the accrual of these grounds, the seller can demand adequate assurance in writing and, absent receipt, "suspend any performance." The securities market offers a great expression which fits the mold of UCC Section 2609: Your first loss is your best loss.

Here is the typical commercial scenario: The seller and buyer enter into a requirements contract that compels the seller to meet the buyer's requirement. A common example is a nationwide chain of specialty restaurants that offer unique entrees (ethnic, organic, theme foods, buffet, or the like). These products are proprietary, which means that the buyer holds trademark, labeling, or formulas or ingredients. Sometimes the products are not proprietary, but very specialized, which means that they not readily available in quantity unless pre-ordered and warehoused by the vendor.

In this scenario, the credit terms are net/60 days. Given a decline in its business fortune (competition, etc.), the buyer defaults in payment of invoices when due, defaults in trade debt owed to other purveyors, and announces precipitous store closings and layoffs. Yet, the buyer places a six figure credit order. Sensing a second default, because the buyer failed to pay the last set of six figure invoices, the seller makes a demand for reasonable assurance before shipping any more products on a credit basis. Facing non delivery of key proprietary product, the buyer is simply "out of luck." The buyer is unable purchase the products from another vendor because the buyer is locked into a requirements contract with the seller. The buyer does not have the cash on hand to purchase from the original vendor. Moreover, the buyer, lacking the funds to pay its seller, does not have the money to pay someone else. No money means no product from anyone.

The buyer is in deep trouble. Requirements contracts offer a secure source for proprietary and specialized products, but entrap the buyer into a brinkmanship should the buyer default and face commercial Armageddon.

How should the buyer survive this head on collision? Before we answer that question, let's define a requirements contract. Typically, a requirements contract is an executory contract. A supply contract, a lease, a licensing agreement for IP, or another contract that is ongoing is an executory contract. An executory contract, even if defaulted but not terminated, is an asset of a bankruptcy estate and subject to the automatic stay. Here is the short answer: "'Contractual rights are intangible property which is included within the definition of the estate of the debtor,'" (*Id.*, quoting *LTV Corp. v. Aetna Cas. & Sur. *401 Co. (In re Chateaugay Corp.)*, 116 B.R. 887, 898 (Bankr.S.D.N.Y.1990). *In re Clearwater Natural Res., LP,* 421 B.R. 392, 400-01 (Bankr. E.D. Ky. 2009). This is serious business, and nobody wants to be the other side of a contempt motion. Appreciating that the requirements contract is an asset of the estate helps better understand the option that would enable the debtor to come up for air as opposed to sinking like a stone. *20,000 Leagues Under the Sea* is not a viable rescue plan for a business.

The sole option here is for the buyer to file Chapter 11. Upon the filing of the Chapter 11, the debtor will come into cash because the debtor ceases paying other past due but non essential creditors. With newly found cash in hand, the debtor can purchase, at least COD, products from its key supplier. Chapter 11 is the best remedy that would enable the debtor to reach products and "get around," a demand for adequate assurance in part. Mind you, the creditor in the Chapter 11 can demand cash in advance, a letter of credit, or other airtight assurance, but at least the debtor is sitting on a pile of other creditors' money.

What happens when the seller has already delivered the goods, but finds out that the buyer is collapsing? Can the seller get back the products, or are the products lost forever? The next chapter discusses reclamation rights that enable the creditor to legally retrieve products in the hand of an insolvent. The rights of reclamation are independent of the rights of secured creditors.

7

Reclamation Rights: Difficult Outcomes in Different Forums (and the Law of the Unexpected)

UCC Code Section 2609 lets the seller lock down the account in order to mitigate any further loss. A reclamation right enables the seller to retrieve goods in the hands of the seller. These two code sections are both sides of the insolvency coin that enables a seller to shrink the footprint of the potential loss. Despite what we see in the movies, under the umbrella of Section 2609 (suspend performance) and Section 2702 (reclaim products), smaller is better.

Let's review for a second. Repetition and review is another form of muscle memory, and memory is everyone's best friend in the event of a commercial emergency. UCC Code 2609 enables a seller to suspend performance, which usually means that the seller can withhold the sale of products on a credit basis. UCC Section 2702 enables a seller to recover the products that were actually delivered to the buyer at a time when the buyer was insolvent. Presumptively (or always) an insolvent buyer is not buyer at all, but a down and out debtor who is about to stumble into a bankruptcy and leave behind a huge trail of obligations.

Commercial Code Section 2702 lets the seller reclaim (repossess) products if they still are in the hands of the buyer as follows:

(1) Where the seller discovers the buyer to be insolvent, he may refuse delivery except for cash including payment for all goods theretofore delivered under the contract, and stop delivery under this division (Section 2705).

(2) Where the seller discovers that the buyer has received goods on credit while insolvent, he may reclaim the goods upon demand made within 10 days after the receipt, but if misrepresentation of solvency has been made to the particular seller in writing within three months before delivery, the 10-day limitation does not apply. Except as provided in this subdivision, the seller may not base a

right to reclaim goods on the buyer's fraudulent or innocent misrepresentation of solvency or of intent to pay.

(3) The seller's right to reclaim under subdivision (2) is subject to the rights of a buyer in ordinary course or other good faith purchaser under this division (Section 2403). Successful reclamation of goods excludes all other remedies with respect to them.

The debtor can file bankruptcy. The seller has reclamation rights under Bankruptcy Code Section 546(c), which provides as follows:

(c)(1) Except as provided in subsection (d) of this section and in section 507(c), and subject to the prior rights of a holder of a security interest in such goods or the proceeds thereof, the rights and powers of the trustee under sections 544(a), 545, 547, and 549 are subject to the right of a seller of goods that has sold goods to the debtor, in the ordinary course of such seller's business, to reclaim such goods if the debtor has received such goods while insolvent, within 45 days before the date of the commencement of a case under this title, but such seller may not reclaim such goods unless such seller demands in writing reclamation of such goods–

(A) not later than 45 days after the date of receipt of such goods by the debtor; or

(B) not later than 20 days after the date of commencement of the case, if the 45-day period expires after the commencement of the case.

(2) If a seller of goods fails to provide notice in the manner described in paragraph (1), the seller still may assert the rights contained in section 503(b)(9).

Reading these statutes and understanding them is important. When a debtor files bankruptcy, makes an assignment for the benefit of creditors, proceeds with a bulk sale, or initiates a "workout" program, the debtor has been purchasing products on credit up to the last moment. When the debtor springs the news of an insolvency or a creditor catches wind of this bad news, every creditor, and their attorneys, crack open the book to see if they can reclaim any of the goods. In mega-bankruptcy cases, the debtor might confront hundreds of reclamation claims, whose dollar amount is more than $100,000,000. In nearly all mega cases, the court issues a special order that lays down the ground for the ruling and allowance of reclamation claims. Typically, these orders will grant administrative priority to these claims, but only on the condition that the vendor continue to sell to the debtor on a credit basis (i.e., standard commercial terms, such as 30 days/net.)

The rights under Bankruptcy Code Section 546(c) offer both less and more to the trade creditors than the UCC. Unlike the 90 days right to reclaim based on the claim of fraud under Commercial Code Section 2702(2), under Bankruptcy Code Section 546(c), the claw back period is only 45 days. UCC Section 2702(2) states in part as follows:

> (2) Where the seller discovers that the buyer has received goods on credit while insolvent he may reclaim the goods upon demand made within *10 days* after the receipt, but if misrepresentation of solvency has been made to the particular seller in writing within three months before delivery the 10-day limitation does not apply.

On the other hand, the reclamation creditor has an administrative claim for goods sold to the insolvent debtor during the *20 days* prior to the filing of the chapter proceeding. This remedy might be hollow if the estate is administratively insolvent. Always keep in mind that a competing secured creditor might gobble up every nickel and render reclamation claims completely worthless. This case offers the bad news:

> Because the reclaimed goods or the proceeds thereof were either liquidated in satisfaction of the Prepetition Indebtedness or pledged to the DIP Lenders pursuant to the DIP Facility, the reclaimed goods effectively were disposed as part of the March 2006 repayment of the Prepetition Credit Facility. Accordingly, the Reclamation Claims are valueless as the goods remained subject to the Prior Lien Defense.

In re Dana Corp., 367 B.R. 409, 421 (Bankr. S.D.N.Y. 2007)

Talk about walking out of court empty handed. Bankruptcy does not create a standalone reclamation right, but only circumscribes the trustee's avoidance powers by the statutory reclamation rights under Commercial Code 2702 (*In re Dana Corp., supra*).

What does this really mean in bankruptcy? Consider this case: The supplier loads up the debtor with a huge shipment worth big money. The day after delivery, the debtor (i.e., the buyer) announces that the debtor is going to file bankruptcy very soon. The supplier immediately delivers a reclamation claim. The debtor files Chapter 11. The debtor gets debtor in possession financing which encumbers all assets of the estate. The supplier's reclamation goods are now collateral securing the post petition financing owed to the DIP financier. If the goods are sold in the ordinary course of business, the funds are gone. While the supplier might have a priority claim, the estate is probably administratively insolvent, or buried under the post petition DIP debt. In the language of the bankruptcy court, the technical answer follows: If the secured debtor consumes the debtor's assets, the reclamation rights are futile because the reclamation rights are subject to "the prior rights of a holder of a security interest in such goods or the proceeds thereof" (11 U.S.C.A. § 546(c)).

Let's compare and contrast with an assignment for the benefit of creditors. An assignment for the benefit of creditor has three players. The first is the debtor, who wants to cease operating a business, transfer assets to a third party, and pay creditors something (or nothing, if the liens exceed the liquidation proceeds). The second is the assignee, who is an independent stake holder who liquidates the assets and pays creditors. The third is the creditors, who might be secured or unsecured. Now, let's consider the case of a debtor loading up on inventory and even exceeding the credit limits with the creditors. With the goods still in hand, the debtor assigns all assets, including the last minute purchases, to the assignee, who will liquidate the products to pay creditors. Creditors who have made a timely demand can recover all goods received by the debtor within 10 days after receipt of the goods. If the financial statement, credit application, or other writing contained a false financial statement (sales, net worth, profit and loss, ownership, equity, retained earnings, ownership of key assets, ongoing business with legacy customer, retention or employment of key personnel, current with vendor, landlord, employees, or taxes), the creditor can recover goods, if sitting on the floor of the debtor, up to 90 days prior to the reclamation notice. If the goods are industrial equipment, rolling stock, trade fixtures, slow moving inventory, or mass ingredients, they might still be intact. If the debtor executes an assignment for the benefit of creditors and has made a false financial statement, the creditor might be able to retrieve these items and stop the assignee from liquidating them. Is this remedy a big deal? You bet. This is a total 100% life saver to the creditor. who can seize the supplier's products from the hands of the assignee. If the assignee is not cooperative, the creditor might have to file suit in order to get a judge to order the assignee to return the reclaimed goods. If the goods are worth millions, this exercise is worth the investment in attorneys' fees, time, and commitment to the process.

Bankruptcy offers different remedies. Bankruptcy law grants priority status to creditors who sell on credit during the 20 days prior to the filing of bankruptcy under Bankruptcy Code Section 503(b)(9). If the goods are still in existence, and a demand has been timely made, the creditor would seek to reclaim the actual goods in the hands of the trustee (if a Chapter 7) or the debtor in possession (if a Chapter 11), or the debtor (if a Chapter 13). Assuming that the debtor is free on a blanket security interest, these creditors could demand that the debtor refrain from selling post petition these goods, and absent cooperation, go to court and seek a restraining order. This is an awful lot of work, but if the goods are worth millions and their recovery would "shrink" the creditor's claim, this foray would be worth the financial investment, time, and energy.

Let's let everyone in the door of real business and leave the textbooks outside for a moment. Here is a dollop of reality. Sales drive wholesale distribution and manufacturing. Without sales, a business would have a half life of about three weeks. This fact means that manufacturers, importers, distributors, and wholesalers only make money when they "move the boxes" or "move the inventory" off their floors. Credit for every hard good manufacturer is a necessity and even a price point. Without credit, most commercial buyers would walk from a sale, or buy what is needed for the here and now. Commercial credit enables buyers to stock inventory and work it down through the terms of the credit. For example, if the credit terms are 60 days (not usual in some industries), the buyer can stock its shelves with product that will likely be "sold down" during the 60 day period. Loading on inventory and selling it down to the date when the invoice is due is just good business. Most commercial credit is 30 to 60 days.

Now, all of this being said, what happens when the seller gets wind of a buyer's faltering financial condition? Sellers tighten up credit terms by ratcheting back credit from 60 days to 15 days. Sellers might reduce the total amount of credit. Sellers might put the buyer on a C.O.D. basis. If the buyer is about to go down the tubes, the seller will be quick to issue a reclamation letter to reclaim the goods, if they exist, on the buyer's docket, inventory, showroom, or other premises. Consider the reclamation letter another arrow in the seller's credit quiver to mitigate the risk of loss. Or, consider large dollar sales a touch like skydiving with two parachutes. The first chute, the main, enables the seller to walk back all credit and stop further credit sales. The second chute is reclamation, which enables the seller to retrieve any inventory within arm's reach.

Sometimes the buyer is completely comatose. All the reclamation letters, telephone calls, emails, and letters don't get the buyer to return the unsold products even though the buyer is about to go out business and has no need for expensive equipment sitting on its dock. If the buyer refuses to return the goods, the remedy is to file suit and seek an ex parte replevin order, which enables the sheriff to break down the door and retrieve the reclaimed goods.

Insiders, Subrogated to Secured Claims or Priority Claims, Wipe Out the Estate

This chapter asks you to take a breather. We are going to revisit common business transactions that, when examined, open doors that allow insiders to exit a disaster without a scratch. These points can seem rudimentary, but correctly identifying the parties peels back layers of uncertainty and confusion.

We start with a debtor that is usually a corporation or limited liability company (LLC). This debtor owns and operates a business that requires cash capital, which is another version of a loan. The lender, which is usually a bank, hard money financier, or private third party, might make the loan but will demand the following:

1. Promissory note executed by the debtor that probably provides for periodic payments. Some loans are lines of credit that permit the debtor to draw down a required amount, but the line of credit comes due on an annual basis.
2. A blanket first lien on the assets of the debtor. This lien might consist of a line on the personal property that consists of the inventory, equipment, lease, receivables, and general intangibles, now owned and hereinafter acquired. If possible, the lender will demand a lien (i.e., deed of trust or mortgage) on the debtor's real property.
3. A personal guaranty by the principal shareholder and spouse. The personal guaranty obligates the guarantors to pay the debt owed by the debtor to the lender in the event that the lender defaults. Nearly every lender (absent some hard money lenders) demands a guaranty. These lenders include the SBA. Hard money-lenders might forgo a personal guaranty if the lender is secured by real property with a deep loan to value ratio that fully secures the lender three or four times.

Absent contractual waivers and in the event of a default, here is the usual outcome. The debtor defaults. The bank has the following options. The bank can foreclose if the security is adequate and readily available. At the same time, the bank will make demands on the guarantor. If the guarantor is solvent and perceives that the security interest might generate full payment of the bank's debt, it might pay the bank in full. As a result of payment in full (interest, penalties, costs, and attorney's fees to date), the guarantor becomes subrogated to the position of the bank. What this means in English is that upon payment, the bank transfers and assigns the note owed by the debtor to the guarantor. The guarantor stands in the position of the bank. The guarantor also holds the secured position of the bank. The expression is that "security follows the debt." The guarantor is now a secured creditor of the debtor.

Let's dig deeper here and explain the transactions in light of the business realities. In making a loan, banks demand security and a personal guaranty. In nearly all cases, the bank takes a blanket lien on the debtor's personal and mortgage in the debtor's real property. The principal of the debtor signs an extensive and detailed personal guaranty. These personal guaranties embody three key waivers: (1) The guarantor waives all rights of subrogation under the guaranty until and unless the bank is paid in full. (2) The debtor cannot repay any direct loans, encumber its assets, or accrue an obligation in favor of, or due to, the principal until and unless the debtor pays the bank in full on its own debt. (3) The guarantor waives the right to compel the bank to foreclose its security first and proceed to seek the deficiency against the guarantor. Presume these waivers. Many banks share standardized "legal language," and their terms are "pre-printed." (The other expression is "carved in stone.")

What do these terms mean in a catastrophic real world default? Typically the bank holds a deed of trust in the debtor's real property, and proceeds with a non judicial sale (i.e., a foreclosure at the courthouse steps), but recovers pennies on the dollar. Given the waiver, the guarantor, more knowledgeable about the real property, has forfeited the right to market the property and, worse, faces the entire liability due the lender. Consider the guarantor a virtual co-debtor or, better stated, a hostage to the bank.

The most common range where the deer and the antelope play in these cases is bankruptcy court—particularly in medium to large dollar cases. What if the guarantor pays off the bank? Under basic subrogation, the guarantor stands in the shoes of the bank, which means that the guarantor is holder and owner of the bank's note, security, and, most importantly, the bank's timely filed proof of claim. The linchpin is Bankruptcy Code Section

509(a), which enables the guarantor to assert the rights of the bank as follows:

> Except as provided in subsection (b) or (c) of this section, an entity that is liable with the debtor on, or that has secured, a claim of a creditor against the debtor, and that pays such claim, is subrogated to the rights of such creditor to the extent of such payment . . .

Here is a good summary of the law:

> Subrogation under § 509(a) allows a guarantor, who pays a debt for which a debtor is primarily liable, to assume the creditor's rights. These rights include any rights to priority distribution or secured status to which the subrogor's claim was entitled.

In re The Med. Shoppe, 210 B.R. 310, 313 (Bankr. N.D. Ill. 1997)

These waivers spell big trouble for the guarantor, who is the target of the bank's ire. Nearly all commercial guaranties make the guaranty a near co-obligor to the bank and not a party secondarily liable, but the guarantor faces the waiver in a shrewdly drafted guaranty. What is the disaster that befalls the guaranty? The answer is that the bank can foreclose on the security, receive pennies on the dollar, and collect the balance from the guarantor. This is bad because the bank under the commercial code and under real property law has the right to foreclose; it probably will exercise limited diligence in generating the "highest and best price" and more likely will take any reasonable offer to liquidate the collateral. Facing this insolvency tsunami, the guarantor forfeits all right to recoup the loss from the debtor and its liquidation proceeds when the trustee, or assignee, liquidates the remaining assets.

The smart money is that the guarantor pays off the bank immediately, stands in the bank's shoes under subrogation, and asserts the secured claim in the insolvency proceedings. With these rights in tow, the guarantor can recover from the debtor's assets (i.e., the collateral) when they are liquidated in a Chapter 7 (or Chapter 11).

What do the unsecured creditors receive, after payment to the subrogated personal guarantor from the estate funds? Pennies or nothing at all, because the personal guarantor stands in the shoes of the bank who had a claim fully secured by all estate assets.

Subrogation also applies if the guarantor (co debtor) pays off priority or administrative debt, taxes, wages, or family law obligations and becomes subrogated to the priority claimants. This includes Chapter 11 administrative debt and tax liabilities, among other claims. Here is the drill:

> In *Standard Oil,* [*Standard Oil,* 330 F.2d at 184] as previously discussed, Standard had paid taxes owed by the debtor and sought to be subrogated to the taxing authorities' priority claim. The court held that because the tax obligation was still subsisting, Standard, as payer of the tax, was entitled to assert the state's priority. *Cf. Harris v. Supreme Plastics, Inc. (In re Supreme Plastics, Inc.),* 8 B.R. 730 (N.D.Ill.1980) (creditor who paid landlord was entitled to landlord's priority but only to a limited extent as a result of other factors not present here).

In re Wingspread Corp., 116 B.R. 915, 931 (Bankr. S.D.N.Y. 1990)

The clever guarantor exits this insolvency debacle nearly unscathed because the security due the bank enables the guarantor to recoup 100% of a potential loss, assuming—a big assumption—that the guarantor acts quickly.

The insider (who is the guarantor) of the debtor has a choice whether to file bankruptcy or execute an assignment for benefit of creditors. If the debtor (usually a corporation) floundered and died because the corporation was undercapitalized, creditors might argue that the subrogated claim of the insider (i.e., the guarantor) (who paid off the bank) should be subordinated to the creditors because the bank loan was disguised capital. What does this mean in English? This means that the insider (who is the guarantor to the bank) formed a shell entity that the insider funded through a big bank loan. The insider did not invest any of his or her own money, but only "borrowed capital" (called "boot strap" capital) because the insider is only investing borrowed money as opposed to the insider own money. Paying the insider, although based on the bank's original loan, might look like a capital distribution when creditors' claims are still unpaid and the insider did not put any of his or her own money in the business. This raises the hackles of the creditors, the trustee, or a creditor's committee, who would blame the insider for the debtor's collapse because the insider failed to adequately capitalize the debtor.

How does this crisis brew to the top? In a bankruptcy, in the face of a motion to transfer the bank's claim to the insider or the insider asserting the bank's security, the creditors or the committee could move to subordinate the insider's claim. These subordination motions are well understood, stand on decades of case law, and are common fodder of reported decisions, treatises, texts, and law review articles. Nobody is reinventing the subordination wheel. The trustee will hold the funds pending the outcome of the subordination litigation. Absent some frivolous claims by the creditors, if the creditors lose, their loss is limited to their own costs and fees in attempting to claim that the insider (the guarantor) should not stand in the shoes of the bank.

An assignment for the benefit of creditors is another kettle of fish. An assignee is a private person who, absent a somebody making a legal stink about the assignee or some misdeeds of the debtor, does not have to answer to a judge. In most states, assignments are not judicial proceedings. Assignees do not need the permission of the creditor to make distributions. An assignee can make whatever disclosures the assignee believes are adequate. An assignee can allow or disallow a claim on its own volition. Assignments do not offer an easy mechanism for creditors to object to insider claims. In fact, the creditors would have to file suit in the state court, restrain distribution of the funds, and post a bond equal to the potential attorney's fee incurred by the assignee in the litigation and the insider. The bond would cover damages. The creditor would personally finance the state court litigation to the bitter end. If the creditor loses the subordination case, the bonding companies would pay fees due the assignee and the insider, which most assuredly would exceed $100,000 each. Based on a credible showing, the bonding company might even pay damages. The creditors, and the creditor's principal, are the indemnitors under the bonds, which means that if the creditor loses the litigation, the creditor has to pay full freight for fees, costs, and damages. Absent the very unusual, this is a complete non starter.

Here is a classic case of the insider legally looting an estate: A business fails. The insider (the guarantor) pays off the bank and stands in the shoes of the bank and therefore can enforce the bank's rights to foreclose on the collateral. Standing in the bank's shoes, the insider forecloses and becomes 100% owner of the debtor's assets.

Alternatively, the debtor can sell itself through a bulk sale, but the insider (now the successor to the bank) can grab 100% of the proceeds as the secured creditor and wipe out the claims of the unsecured creditors. Neat trick. Chances are good that nobody would make a peep.

Let's get back to an assignment. If the insider (the guarantor) paid off the bank, the insider can immediately put the debtor through an assignment and have the assignee liquidate the assets and turn over all cash to the insider. No muss and no fuss because the assignee can consummate the transaction without notice to anyone, including the creditors.

Bankruptcy

The Short Story

Synopsis

The U.S. Constitution authorized the creation of the United States Bankruptcy Court, which is an adjunct to the United States District Court. Bankruptcy is a body of federal law. Bankruptcy Courts are in each state, presided over by bankruptcy judges, who have core jurisdiction over bankruptcy and related matters. In some cases, the judges apply state law.

Consumers typically file Chapter 7 (liquidation), Chapter 11 (small business), and Chapter 13 (wage earner or small business). Farmers file Chapter 12. Governments file Chapter 9. The overarching theme of bankruptcy is that the debtor surrenders him or herself to the jurisdiction of the court, pledges fidelity and honesty in all disclosures, turns over non exempt property, and obtains a discharge from debts.

Bankruptcy is a specialized legal process that requires research, knowledge of the rules of procedure, and great attentiveness to detail. Attorneys must read every piece of paper that comes from the parties or the court. Common errors are too common.

Legal Basis

Title 11 of the United States Code, the Bankruptcy Rules of Procedure, the Federal Rules of Civil Procedure, and 28 U.S.C 157 seq.

Bankruptcy has created a very large body of law. The bankruptcy bibliography offers an endless buffet of case reporters, treatises, practice guides, academic articles, and magazines.

When Do I File a Claim?

90 days from the date of the First Meeting of Creditors, or the date specific in the FMC notice or notice to file proofs of claims.

Objections to claims of exemption are due 30 days after the first meeting. Actions to bar the discharge or exempt the debt from the discharge is 60 days from the date of the first meeting. Deadlines to oppose motions are set by statute, rule, or local rules, or they are specified in the moving papers. These are dates certain. Errors are fatal.

What Does It Mean to File a Claim?

If you are an authorized Electronic Case Filing (ECF) user, file through ECF. Always get confirmation of the filing in the right case. If you are not an ECF filer, use personal delivery, overnight services, or USPS Express mail.

How Do I Locate the Filing?

Easy. The filing is available on PACER, or you can contact the local bankruptcy court or search by other means, using Westlaw, Lexis Nexus, and other commercial search services.

What Do I File?

The Proof of Claim form required by the court. The clerk might accept a non conforming form, but this is a big risk. The court's forms are readily available online. Always insure that you have filed in the right case given that larger cases might encompass multiple case numbers and different estates. Failing to file in the right case is a common and expensive error, but it is avoidable with diligence.

Do I Get Accruing Interest?

Yes, for secured claims to the date of payment, if the secured creditor is over secured. No, for unsecured creditors, unless it is a solvent estate.

Do I Need to Update the Claim?

Yes, if there is a change in circumstances or in the amount.

Who Gets the Claim?

The court, the court appointed claims depository, or many third parties. Watch for instructions on mega cases and particularly for the filing of administrative claims under Bankruptcy Code Section 503(b)(9) (regarding goods sold to the debtor, but unpaid, within 20 days prior to the filing).

What Should I Include?

Everything. Given that bankruptcy cases can span years, or even a decade, make sure that the claim is very complete as records might be lost over the years. Be thorough.

Are There Privacy Issues?

Redact social security numbers, driver's licenses, bank account numbers, and other clearly private information. This is a very big deal. Errors are very painful.

What Should I Expect from the Court and Other Parties?

If you are electronically filing a claim, your receipt is the fact that the docket shows your filing online and on time. If you are paper filing, you should get a return copy that bears a filing stamp.

File a request for special notice. You will receive electronic or paper copies of everything that is filed. Sometimes you are required to participate in the plan, claim objections, responding to lien avoidance motions, etc. Read the mail—bankruptcy traps the unwary or inattentive person. Plans always offer booby traps.

Is There Judicial Supervision?

Extensive. These cases are very detail driven. The U.S. Trustee likewise supervises the cases.

Is There a Risk of Side Deals?

Prior to filing, the debtor and relatives connive to hide or retitle property, record false deeds of trust, or manufacture false notes. Prior to filing, assets are sold at unjustifiably low stated prices, while additional proceeds are paid to the buyer "under the table" and in cash. During the proceedings, the risk of a side deal is substantially diminished given, for example, the fact that sales are court approved and supervised in part by the U.S. Trustee.

Are There Statutory Safeguards against Fraud?

The Bankruptcy Code at many levels seeks to eradicate fraud. The U.S. Trustee is vigilant. However, many schedules and statements of affairs, motion papers filed by the debtor, and other claims are skewed in favor of the debtor; they contain omissions, half truths, and outright falsehoods. Creditors bear the burden of reviewing the filings and reporting errors to the trustee or the U.S. Trustee or initiating action themselves.

Can Another Party Object to My Claim?

The trustee, the debtor, and others might object to your claim. The trustee or the debtor is the usual party.

If There Is an Objection, What Happens?

Respond timely to the claim objection, prove up your case, and appear at all hearings.

What Does the Trustee Provide at Close?

The trustee provides a detailed accounting of receipts and disbursements, payments to priority creditors and secured creditors, and payments to creditors if money is left over.

What Are the Priorities?

Taxes, wages, trustees' fees and expenses, attorneys' fees and expenses, secured claims, Perishable Agricultural Commodities Act (PACA) claims, statutory priorities, landlords' claims (maybe), U.S. government claims, family support obligations, and—finally—unsecured creditors.

Do I Have an Obligation to Object to Another Claim?

You might have standing to object.

When Can I Object?

Sooner rather than later. Be attentive to the proceedings.

Do I Have Remedies if a Bad Claim Has Been Filed?

Raise the dickens with the debtor, the trustee, or the U.S. Trustee, or file a motion.

What About Accuracy of Claims and Liability?

Claims must be very accurate. Avoid exaggeration or inflation. A claim is not a personal injury lawsuit in which the creditor can ask for the moon. Ask for what is owed.

Is Compliance with FDCPA Required?

Maybe—it depends on the local federal court rulings on this issue. (FDCPA includes an entire body of federal and state consumer protection law.)

When Do I See an Accounting or Money?

At close of the case, which is anywhere between 12 and 60 months.

When Should I Expect Payment?

In 12 to 60 months.

How Is Transparency?

Fair to good because many debtors' filings are inaccurate or even purposely falsified. Creditor filings are slightly, but not much, better. Bankruptcy is highly adversarial.

What Are Some Other Options?

State court dissolutions or receiverships.

Stay of Legal Proceedings?

Yes—for all actions against the debtor or a person holding estate property.

Guarantor Status?

Sue the guarantor.

Overall Fairness?

These are well established statutory proceedings which are necessarily fair.

Right to Declare an Exemption?

Yes.

Right of Reclamation?

Bankruptcy Code Section 546 preserves the right of reclamation for goods sold within 10 days. Bankruptcy Code Section 503(b)(9) gives creditors a priority of payment for goods sold on credit within 20 days prior to the filing of the bankruptcy. These rights encourage vendors to sell to an insolvent given some assurance of payment should the debtor file bankruptcy, but if the debtor is buried under pre or post petition debt, reclamation creditors get nothing.

What Are My Proactive Strategies?

Few bankruptcies are a bolt out of the blue. However, given the right of a claw back (i.e., a preference under Bankruptcy Code Section 547(b)), pro-active remedies are limited. Any liens and levies older than 90 days will survive.

Personal guaranties provide some hope of payment. Be vigilant in reset-ting credit or lender terms; a perfected security interest might enable the creditor to participate as a secured creditor and collect everything, assum-ing equity in the property. File the claim timely and read and respond to all papers that you receive. Always request special notice.

Many Chapter 11s and 13s are dismissed, but some refile. You must refile the proof of the claim in the new case. Claims for goods sold within 20 days are entitled to priority under Section 503(b)(9) and maybe other reclamation rights. PACA claims take priority.

The Long Story

The Cutting Room Floor

The short story leaves some stuff on the cutting room floor, including non case dispositive asset sales, debtor in possession financing, motion to allow administrative claims, motion to retain counsel, all fee motions, motions to allow use of cash collateral, compromise of controversies, and motion to dismiss or convert a case. These motions are important to the parties. Some motions, such as a motion to convert or dismiss, can alter the outcome of the case. In its effort to enable a non specialist to navigate through bankruptcy and emerge unscathed, this book leaves these topics aside.

History and Case Law of Bankruptcy

Bankruptcy case law is extensive. The Westlaw *Bankruptcy Law Reporter* publishes bankruptcy judge opinions, district court opinions on bankruptcy matters, bankruptcy appellate panel opinions, the circuit court of appeals opinions, and, of course, U.S. Supreme Court opinions. In addition, state courts, U.S. tax courts, and other courts might have concurrent jurisdictions on certain bankruptcy issues and accordingly render an opinion. Since 1978, the American Bankruptcy Institute has published a well researched monthly journal. The major law reviews offer many annual offerings on key bankruptcy issues.

A brief history of bankruptcy law highlights its peaks and valleys. They include the enactment of the 1898 Bankruptcy Act, which was amended in 1938. The core of the 1898 Act was summary or plenary jurisdiction. The Bankruptcy Reform Act of 1978 offered the modern Bankruptcy Code, which ostensibly abolished the difference between plenary and summary jurisdiction and which converted bankruptcy judges into *de facto* Article III judges. *Northern Pipeline Construction vs. Marathon Pipe Line Company* (1982) 458 U.S. 50 rolled back the "plenary jurisdiction" of the bankruptcy court on the basis that only an Article III judge could exercise jurisdiction over non bankruptcy matters. In response, Congress passed The Bankruptcy Amendment and Federal Judgeship Act of 1984, which rewrote the judge's jurisdiction. In 1986, Congress enacted a permanent U.S. Trustee System as the watchdog for all participants; additional amendments passed in 1994.

The biggest change is the Bankruptcy Abuse Prevention and Consumer Protection Act of 2005, which channeled high earners into Chapter 13s, made debtors' attorneys more vigilant in the filing of accurate schedules and statements of affairs, and generally enhanced creditors' rights. Probably the most important Supreme Court case is *Stern vs. Marshall* (2011) 564 U.S. 2, which precluded bankruptcy judges from entering final judgments on "non-core matters."

Important Dates

Bankruptcy is date driven. These dates are jurisdictional, which means that (a) the failure to file forever extinguishes a right and (b) the court cannot restore that right no matter the excuse (maybe and most likely). It precludes a party from any relief based on "excusable neglect, inadvertence or surprise" found generally in Bankruptcy Rule 9024, which incorporates FRCP 60(b).

Late is fatal. Judges consider late filed trial briefs and oppositions to motions. Appellate courts set aside a default in the filing of transcripts and briefs. On the other hand, bankruptcy is unforgiving. *Miss the date, blow the case.* Bankruptcy is the graveyard of inexperienced attorneys.

What are the sources of the dates? This is important because bankruptcy law is more than a single "code" book, akin to state statutes, court rules, and administrative regulations (similar to the Code of Federal Regulations, or CFR). Bankruptcy law consists of Title 11 of the U.S. Code (the Bankruptcy Code); 28 USC 157 seq.; the Federal Rules of Bankruptcy Procedure; the local rules of the district; sometimes the local rules of the U.S. District Court; the Federal Rules of Civil Procedures, which generally apply in adversary and contested proceedings; the local rules of the particular court in the district; and the rules (i.e., the standing orders) of the judge, which are usually online. The bankruptcy court adjudicates secured transactions (Article 9 of the UCC and real property security), judgments liens and levies (local state enforcement law), PACA, the Employee Retirement Income Security Act (ERISA), federal and state tax laws, and local laws. "Drop dead dates" flow from all these sources.

Below are the most common dates, but other dates abound. You will get more out of this section if you have a copy of the bankruptcy code in hand or online.

30 days from the date of the first meeting of creditors (FMC): Object to debtor's exemptions under Bankruptcy Rule 4003(b)(1).

60 days from the FMC: File a non dischargeability action under Bankruptcy Code Section 523(c) and Bankruptcy Rule 4007(c), for fraud, breach of fiduciary duty, and willful and malicious conduct. Section 523(a)(2),(4) and (6) or action to bar the discharge under

Bankruptcy Code Section 727(a)(2),(3),(4),(5),(6) or (7). If not, the discharge will be entered, which dissolves the automatic stay and invokes the permanent injunctions under Section 524(a)(1).

90 days from the FMC: File a proof of claim, unless the court provides another dates, assuming the case is originally a no-asset case under Bankruptcy Code Section 3003(c). Filing the proof of claim means getting the proof of claim filed on time. Post PACER, the creditor can electronically file the proof of claim. Avoid waiting until the last date to file the proof of claim. This is a formula for an unforced error. First, something might go wrong, including a power outage, which is common in the Midwest during the winter, or the administrative assistants who are the actual "e-filers" might be unexpectedly absent. Next, getting the claim on file and requesting special notice enables the creditor to follow the proceeding from the outset. Bankruptcies tend to go "in like a lion, out like a lamb." Note: At the outset of the case, the judge presides over the asset sales, cash collateral motions, debtor in possession financing, and, of course, the voluminous first day motions. In mega cases, the court would consider 30 to 40 (or more) first day motions, which are routinely granted as they enable the debtor to kick off the case.

30 day life of the automatic stay for the second bankruptcy filed within one year under Bankruptcy Code Section 362(c)(3)(A): This rule gives the creditor an opportunity to overcome the automatic stay. The third serial bankruptcy is the charm because the debtor forfeits the automatic stay.

20 and 45 day rule for reclamation of goods (aside from 503(b)(9) rights): "a seller of goods that has sold goods to the debtor...if the debtor has received such goods while insolvent, within 45 days before the date of the commencement of a case under this title, but such seller may not reclaim such goods unless such *seller demands in writing reclamation* of such goods—(A) not later than **45** days after the date of receipt of such goods by the debtor; or (B) not later than **20** days after the date of commencement of the case, if the 45-day period expires after the commencement of the case." The rights are frequently overlooked, but are very important because they elevate a pre petition into an administrative creditor who is an entity with priority of payment. However, the creditor might have to file a "live" notice of motion and have a hearing on the claim to insure payment. Filing the proof of claim might be inadequate.

20 days prior to the filing of the bankruptcy: If goods were delivered during this period, this entitles the creditor to file an administrative claim under Section 503(b)(9).

14 days, or whatever time is designated in the notice, prior to the date for a hearing to oppose a motion: The time to respond to a contested matter, which is the sale of property, motion to avoid a judicial lien, etc., is set by local rules. These notices set forth in detail the date when the response is due.

30 days to respond to an adversary proceeding complaint under Bankruptcy Rule 7012(a).

30 days to respond to a claim objection under Bankruptcy Rule 3007(c).

14 days to file an appeal for an adverse ruling on a contested matter or adversary (or just about anything else under Bankruptcy Code Section 8002(a)(1)).

14 days to file a motion for reconsideration under Bankruptcy Rule 9023. (Rule 9023 is subject to the same limitations under FRCP 59(e).)

14 day stay on order granting motion for relief from the automatic stay (Bankruptcy Rule 4003(c)). Acting too soon might violate the automatic stay and might earn the creditor and creditor's attorney a contempt of court charge. Always ask for a waiver of the 14 days.

7 days to serve by mail an adversary summons and complaint (Bankruptcy Rule 7004(e)). This is very important. This is a small window. Attentiveness to detail is paramount. This is a rule frequently botched by attorneys. It is one of those "drop what you are doing and do this now" rules.

60 days for the Chapter 7 trustee to assume or reject an executory contract (IP license, lease of real or personal property, etc.)

90 day exposure for a preference transfer (i.e., money or property paid to a creditor on account of antecedent debt) under Bankruptcy Code Section 547(c).

1 year exposure for a preference transfer if the transferee is an insider under Bankruptcy Code Section 547(b)(4)(B) and Section 1010(31).

180 days to revoke a Chapter 11 plan under Bankruptcy Code Section 1144.

1 year to file an action to revoke the debtor's discharge under Bankruptcy Code Section 727(e)—but read the *fine* print.

2 year statute of limitation to file a preference, fraudulent conveyance and actions by the trustee (but subject to equitable tolling) under Bankruptcy Code Section 546(a)(1)(A).

Scream or Die: Instead of setting every dispute on the court's active "law and motion calendar," a party can file a motion that requires that within 21 days (check the local rule) an aggrieved individual must file and serve an objection to the motion, supported by a memorandum of points and authorities and declarations or other evidence. (This is the correct title for these motions.)

Dates incorporated into Plan and Disclosure Statement regimes: In all large scale cases, the court imposes dates when objections to disclosure statements and plan objections are due. These are dates certain. These orders compel service upon the debtor, the attorneys for the debtor, the committee attorney, the U.S. Trustee, the major secured creditors, and others. The order requires service by fax, email, or overnight.

Dates incorporated into Chapter 13 FMC notice to object to plan: In some districts, the FMC notice sets the date for filing objections to the proposed plan. The typical scenario is that the plan objections are due on the date of the FMC or sometime after the FMC. These are dates that are certain.

Large Scale Reclamation Claim Regimes: In large scale retail grocery, food, manufacturing, or other cases that involve trade debt for goods, many creditors bombard the debtor with viable reclamations claims under Bankruptcy Code Section 546 and Commercial Code Section 2702. The court issues a date specific order that requires the timely filing of reclamation claims. These regimes are very specific, requiring, again, tremendous attention to detail.

8 years: The debtor cannot receive another discharge for 8 years after a prior discharge under Bankruptcy Code Section 727(a)(9).

The anecdotal narrative of malpractice committed in bankruptcy is full of missing dates and failing to grasp the significance of the plans, including the failure to object to the discharge of third party (i.e., non debtor) under a personal guaranty.

The Bankruptcy Code offers other dates which requires slavish attention to detail. Unlike civil litigation, which bears some elasticity, depending upon the judge, dates drive a bankruptcy case. Without the necessity of a formal motion, a bankruptcy judge will dismiss *sue sponte* a late filed non dischargeability proceeding.

What Is the Bankruptcy Court?

The bankruptcy court is an adjunct of the district court. A bankruptcy case is technically filed in the district court, but referred to the bankruptcy court to adjudicate all matters. Absent the unusual, the bankruptcy court will resolve all matters brought before it, except (1) personal injury and wrongful death cases; (2) cases subject to abstention (state law battle in progress); (3) cases where the reference has been withdrawn, which are typically state and federal law claims (with a jury trial demand attached) that are non-core.

A creditor can move to withdraw the reference for the purpose of having the district court hear some portion of the case. The standard fare of a withdraw motion are claims to or against the debtor, arising out of a non bankruptcy body of law, including antitrust, property damage, personal injury, securities, maritime and admiralty claims, or claims that invoke a jury trial right. The most common are personal injury claims, which are guaranteed by 28 USC 157(b)(5):

> The district court shall order that personal injury tort and wrongful death claims shall be tried in the district court in which the bankruptcy case is pending, or in the district court in the district in which the claim arose, as determined by the district court in which the bankruptcy case is pending.

Bankruptcy court is not an administrative court conducted by an administrative law judge (ALJ). ALJs adjudicate workers' compensations benefits, social security, maritime disputes, trademark and patent battles, the entire gamut of employment disputes, and other regulatory or even civil matters. The rulings by the ALJ bind the parties, but the ALJ ruling is enforceable when reduced to a civil judgment in a court of competent jurisdiction.

On the other hand, bankruptcy court, as part of the district court, can render a final money judgment (assuming *Stern vs. Marshall* jurisdiction), which enables the judgment creditor to enforce the judgment. The bankruptcy court (clerk's office, to be exact) will issue writs of execution, abstracts of judgment, and other routine processes. Bankruptcy judges will conduct a debtor's examination, issue post judgment relief, and, if need be, hold the debtor in contempt for the failure to comply with a turnover order.

Jury Trial Rights and *Stern vs. Marshall* Jury Trial Rights

Stern vs. Marshall held that the bankruptcy judge cannot enter a final judgment on a state law claim that is the province of an Article III judge. Absent consent, the bankruptcy judge could act as a magistrate judge and issue findings that the District Court would review, de novo, to adopt, reject, modify, or enter a new and different judgment.

Stern vs. Marshall has led to an explosion of motion to withdraw the reference on certain matters (i.e., non-core cases) to the district court. *Stern vs. Marshall* is an ecological disaster. Brazil has been clear cut to meet the printing demand for law review articles that explain this case.

Investing Money, Time, Effort, and Energy in a Case: What Do You Get?

Bankruptcy litigation is time consuming, detail driven, and technical. Everything is date certain. Bankruptcy judges produce their own opinions, which wind their way into *West's Bankruptcy Reporter*. Most consumer bankruptcies are "no assets" cases. Most Chapter 13s and 11s produce a modest dividend. Of course, some bankruptcies might generate 100% payment to creditor, but these cases are rare.

Generally, attorneys for the trustee, the creditor's committee in big cases, those who represent secured creditors, and attorneys for the debtor earn their keep and produce results.

Important Notices and Junk Mail

The debtor, the court, and other parties churn out notices of hearings, proposed plans, "scream or die" notices, notices of discharges, notices of dismissal, etc. Creditors complain about the volume of notices. Some notices are important and others are not. Mind you, the notice of an asset sale is critical to a secured creditor holding a lien but unimportant to a creditor holding a small unsecured debt. Notice of the hearing on fees is important to creditors holding large claims, competing administrative claimants, or secured creditors who might bear exposure under Bankruptcy Code 506(c) (exposure for fees that arise from the "preserving, or disposing of the collateral"). The importance of a notice depends upon whose ox is getting gored, or, better stated: No ox, no gore.

Notices come in 31 flavors or more, but these notices are probably the most important.

First Meeting of Creditors Notice (FMC)

This is the most important notice in the entire case. The FMC advises of the bankruptcy, which immediately imposes the automatic stay (stop what you are doing); the date to file the proofs of claims, if an asset case; the date to object to the exemptions; the date to file the non dischargeability action or action to bar the discharge; the correct names of the debtor, the debtor's attorney, and the trustee; and the date, time, and place of the first meeting of creditors.

The creditor should carefully note the case number and type of case, which itself has repercussions downstream. Insure that the creditor can locate the "credit" or "collection file" associated with the precise debtor. Some names are common. Worse, the creditor might maintain a file under the name of HARRY'S BAR AND GRILL when the true name of the debtor is 1001 MAIN STREET WATERING HOLE OF TUSCALOOSA ALABAMA, LLC.

Many FMCs list the case as "no asset," which means that the creditor need not file a claim unless the court sends out a notice to creditors to file proofs of claims. Here is the trick. A creditor receives notice of the proceeding because the debtor has listed the creditor in the schedules and the mailing matrix. Absent the most bizarre events, the court and parties will send out notices to the creditors. But some debtors are every clever. The debtor will not list the creditor, but will provide notice, which might even include a phone call, a mailed copy of the FMC, or a notice in the state court collection actions. Given the mailing matrix does not list the creditor, the creditor might not receive the second notice from the court that solicits creditors to file a proof of claim.

The antidote to this trick is to file a request for special notice with the court that compels the courts and the parties to provide the creditor with the notice. The courts do not impose a fee or charge to file a request for special notice, which itself is a one page document.

The First Meeting of Creditors: A Quick Tour

The court schedules a first meeting of creditors, which enables the trustee and the creditors to interrogate the debtor under oath. In a consumer Chapter 7, the trustee conducts the hearing, which lasts about ten minutes. The creditor is allotted about five minutes to quiz the debtor. The hearings are tape recorded. The office of the U.S. Trustee provides a digital copy of the FMC. Chapter 7 FMCs are busy spectacles.

In a Chapter 11, and depending upon the court, the U.S. Trustee might conduct the hearing in part but let the creditors carry the ball. These proceedings can last for hours, depending upon the case's complexity and the interest or status of the creditors (i.e., banks, labor unions, plaintiffs in lawsuit, major creditors, and governmental entities). Depending on the case, these FMCs compel the debtor to answer virtually any questions about its liabilities and assets in a forum. Again the U.S. Trustee records the testimony, which is reduced to a CD available for free or a modest charge.

The failure of the debtor to appear might result in the dismissal of the case or the denial of the debtor's discharge. The U.S. Trustee or the creditor can compel the debtor to bring records at the first meeting.

The bankruptcy judge does not preside over the first meeting of creditors. The U.S. Trustee generally "presides" over the first meeting of creditors, but neither the U.S. Trustee nor the Chapter 7 or 13 trustee have adjudicatory power. In Chapter 13s, which have their own calendar, the Chapter 13 trustee presides. In a Chapter 7, the Chapter 7 trustee presides. In some cases, the trustee will employ an assistant who actually conducts the hearing.

Bankruptcy Rule 2004: Examine the Debtor and Produce Records

A party in interest (usually a creditor) can compel the debtor to appear for a more lengthy examination and produce records under Bankruptcy Rule 2004. These examinations explore the debtor's assets and liabilities and potential bankruptcy claims. If the creditor is considering a non dischargeability action, or the trustee needs additional information before suing third parties for a turnover of assets, fraudulent conveyances, or preferences, examining the debtor at the outset is a first rate head start. Every dollar collected by the trustee pays, after the top tier administrative fees and expenses, non dischargeable taxes owed to the IRS and state. Appreciating the potential payment of the taxes, the debtor willingly provides information that would enable the trustee to marshal assets, when liquidated, that would pay the debtor's taxes.

In significant cases, the major creditors, the creditor's committee, banks, labor unions, and other interested parties examine the debtor through Rule 2004 examinations.

A Rule 2004 examination order likewise enables the creditor to reach records in the hands of third parties through a subpoena. Federal subpoenas have a significant reach. A examination succeeds with current records in hand, but stick to the subpoenas, examinations, and public record search. Depending upon the circuit, the Federal and possibly state Fair Debt Collection Practice Acts apply in Bankruptcy Court. The Fair Credit Reporting Act might apply. Always remember that using surreptitious means to locate a bank account is illegal under the Gramm–Leach–Bliley Act (GLBA), also known as the Financial Services Modernization Act of 1999. The act limits the methods and means of unearthing information.

In large cases, the use of Rule 2004 is very common.

Notice to File Proof of Claim

A little background helps. Nearly 90% of consumer bankruptcies are "no-asset cases," which relieves the clerk's office of management of proofs of claim. The vast majority of filings are electronic: nonetheless, the clerk's office still administers paper proofs of claim. Most FMCs instruct creditors that the case is "no asset" and therefore no proof of claim is required. Conversely, should money come into the case, the clerks send out these notices.

These are dates certain, which means that the creditor must comply or forfeit, absent the most extenuating circumstances, the right to participate in the case.

In very large Chapter 11 cases, the court will send out a special order that designates the claim bar date along with a blank proof of claim; it will designate a claims administrator other than the court, who is the filing entity for the proofs of claims. This is an expectation. You have to file in paper form, unless accepted electronically, the proof of claim with the "claims agent," who in turn will provide you with a post card that acknowledges receipt of the proof of claim. These claims agents offer electronic access to their dockets, which likewise confirm the filing of the proofs of claim, and provide, for free, a copy of what was filed. These claims agents are adjuncts to the court. Timely filing of the proofs of claims is paramount.

Be very alert to new case numbers given the risk of serial filings.

After the claim has been filed, exit the court's website, but reopen the court's website again to locate the case and the claim's register. Confirm that the proof of claim actually filed in the right case and right case number. Download the "filed" proof of claim. Many large cases include a dozen or more separate filings, with separate case numbers. These case numbers are sequential, which invites errors. Closing and reopening the court's website to confirm the viable filings *in the right case* offers the "last clear chance" to avoid a filing error.

Notice of Dismissal of the Bankruptcy

Few Chapter 7s are dismissed. On the other hand, many Chapter 13s are dismissed at any time given the debtor's default in making plan payments, failing to timely prosecute a confirmable plan, or failing to file schedules and statements of affairs, along with rafts of other key documents. Statistics vary, but the percentage for dismissal might equal or exceed 50%. Some Chapter 11s are dismissed for the same reasons and with a big percentage.

Upon the dismissal of the case, you are free to enforce the judgment or claim, file suit, seize assets, levy bank accounts, or terminate licenses, leases, or other rights. The downside is that the debtor who filed any type of bankruptcy before (and was dismissed) is inclined to file bankruptcy again when pressed. It is fair expectation the debtor will file another bankruptcy after the first case is dismissed.

Let's stop the show for a second. Bankruptcy #1 has gone down the drain. The stay is lifted. The creditor is free to collect, with aggressive enforcement.

Expect another bankruptcy, which offers a new FMC and new case number. The second bankruptcy is a brand new case with a new case number, new dates, and different repercussions based on pre petition conduct, such as preferences and other transfers. The number one error is failing to use the new case number for filing a proof of claim in the new case. (Do not use the case number from the dismissed proceeding.)

Before launching enforcement, examine the docket to see if the debtor has sought to rescind the prior dismissal order. Based on good cause, the bankruptcy judge is inclined to vacate the dismissal order and reinstate the original proceedings. An action taken in between might (or might not) be valid. Moreover, if the court vacates the dismissal order, the court would reinstate the automatic stay, which would bar further enforcement. Absent a request for special notice and electronic access to the court, the creditor could get notice only through the mails, which might delay actual notice that the judge rescinded the prior dismissal.

In Chapter 13s, debtors have a tendency to refile after the first case is dismissed. You should oppose the motion to rescind the dismissal of the first case if in fact you have effectively levied on the debtor's assets post dismissal. Chances are good that the court might deny the motion to rescind, which forces the debtor to file a new case, which means that the automatic stay starts upon the filing of the second case only.

You are not out of the woods. The levy, lien, enforcement, or collection between the two cases is still vulnerable to a claw-back (i.e., a preference claim under Section 547(b)).

Notice of Discharge

This is a seminal moment in the bankruptcy case. The discharge order frees the debtor of all pre-petition liabilities (with certain exceptions) that include fraud, breach of fiduciary duty, or willful and malicious conduct. This is a big deal to the debtor, assuming that the creditor did not timely file a lawsuit to exempt the debt from the discharge. A notice of discharge is the fresh start offered by the bankruptcy court.

The notice of discharge also extinguishes the automatic stay, which the permanent discharge replaces. Only debts are discharged and not valid liens, which encumber the debtor's real or personal property. These liens pass unaffected by the discharge. A creditor can seek to proceed with foreclosure under the lien, even though the unsecured debt is discharged.

That the discharge does not extinguish a judgment lien on the debtor's real property usually comes a shock to the debtor. To avoid the lien, the debtor must reopen the bankruptcy (which is routinely granted) and move to avoid the lien if impairing the homestead exemption (see below).

Notice of Hearing (or Motion) to Avoid Judicial Lien Impairing Homestead

Bankruptcy Section 522(b)(1) permits the court to "exempt from property of the estate the property listed [in the section]." What does this mean in English? The debtor may exit bankruptcy with all exempt property in hand in order that the debtor can "start fresh." Exempt property, or some dollar value attached to property, is immune from enforcement by a creditor. As a one paragraph primer, exempt property comes in three flavors:

1. Property immune from enforcement, such as social security, pension plans, or disability payments under federal or state law, without the necessity of the debtor filing a claim of exemption. This includes real property in Florida and Texas.
2. Property immune from enforcement but in which the debtor must file a claim of exemption to demonstrate immunity from any enforcement.
3. A dollar amount of value in the property that is immune from enforcement, such as $7,500.00 for tools of the trade, equity in a car, heirlooms, jewelry, or artwork, or $50,000 plus (depends on the state) in real property.

Generally these exemptions consist of the state law exemptions, or a grubstake (fixed dollar exemption) allowed by state law or bankruptcy law under Bankruptcy Code Section 522(d). In nearly all cases, unsecured creditors have little interest in these motions given their granting, or denial, rarely products a big return. On the other hand, a creditor holding a judgment lien (abstract of judgment) might forfeit the lien on the house if the judgment lien impairs the homestead.

Let me simplify this unduly detail driven body of law. Assume that the debtor owns a $1,000,000 home with a $500,000 mortgage. Assume that the homestead is $100,000.00. The debtor has $400,000 in equity above the homestead. The judgment is $200,000.00. The debtor cannot avoid the lien because the debtor will emerge from bankruptcy with the $100,000 homestead rights intact.

On the other hand, assume that the first mortgage is $900,000.00, and the homestead is $100,000.00. The $200,000 judgment impairs the homestead. The court would vacate the lien.

The value of the property is determined as of the date of filing bankruptcy. Real property values are subject to appraisals. Appraisers might offer wildly conflicting appraisals at the hearings to avoid liens. Sometimes the validity and amount of the senior liens are in dispute. Even junior consensual liens might be fraudulent if owed to family members or friends. This is very common. Whether the debtor owns the property as community property, joint tenancy, separate property, tenants in common, a partnership, or by some other arrangement is also a common battle.

After this one page introduction, you can see that motions to avoid liens have many "moving parts," and require slavish attention to detail. Without denigrating the bankruptcy bar, many debtors file motions to avoid liens that lack factual support, offer an absurdly low value of the property, or claim that senior or junior liens are valid, when they are ostensibly fraudulent. Given the expenses, effort, and skill needed to oppose these motions, some secured creditors "walk from the table" and let the liens go by default. If the cost to litigate the lien is $2,500.00 (a common number), the lien balance is $5,000.00, and there is no guaranty of success, most judgment creditors would abandon the lien or settle for a lien reduction. These are hypothetical numbers; the risk and reward factors are paramount in assessing whether to joust over liens and real estate values. Money, shall we say, is money.

Notice of Hearing (or Motion) Objecting to a Proof of Claim

A creditor may file a proof of claim that seeks payment if funds are available after payment of secured, administrative, and priority creditors. Let's break up this sentence as follows:

A.   The creditor has to file the claim with the clerk of the court, or a claim's agent, before the bar date.

B.   The claim must set forth a specific dollar amount, the basis of the claim, attach supporting documents that evidence the liability of the debtor, state whether the claim is secured or unsecured, and indicate any priority. If the claim is administrative (i.e., incurred during the case, or goods old within 20 days prior to the filing under Section 503(b)(9)), the creditor might be required to file a motion with the court. Clarity and simplicity is king.

C.   The claim must prove up a contract, tort, or other viable claim.

D.   The trustee will only make payment if funds are available after payment of secured, priority, and administrative claims. In many, or even most, cases, all estate proceeds are paid to senior creditors. Pennies on the dollar is common.

E.   The trustee, debtor, or any other party in interest can object to the claim.

The best practice is to attach all supporting documents to prove up the claim in order to avoid objections based on a "lack of documentation." Many disputed proofs of claims are settled after some haggling. The paramount issue is to determine what percentage is paid to creditors. If the case is paying 10% on the dollar, good business judgment suggests aggressive bargaining lest the attorneys' fee to litigate the claim exceed any recovery.

The trustee (or debtor) serves claim objections by mail. The address for the mailing is the address on the proof of claim, which requires the creditor (or the attorney) to update the address in the event of a change of address or move. Sometimes, the trustee will object to 50 to 100 or even more claims at once. This is a big problem because some creditors (or their attorneys) lack a familiarity with an omnibus claim objection (this is the title) and might not readily identify the claim object that applies to them.

Even if the creditor ferrets out of the voluminous paperwork the objection to its claim, the creditor has to further ferret out the basis of the objection. Worse, in large cases, the claim objection requires timely service of an opposition to the claim objection, which is filed electronically, that the objecting party receive notice, along with attorneys for other interested parties. While the paperwork in response to the claim objection is not too overwhelming, getting the response filed on time and serving all interested parties can be burdensome. Likewise, in large cases, the debtor (i.e., the reorganized debtor) hires a third party claim administrator or specialized law firm, who undertake the claim analysis and objections. Claimants respond to claim objections morning, noon, and night, but for the first time filer, this can be a laborious task.

Do not wait to the last moment to respond given the time sensitive requirements of filing.

Consider the proof of claim a surrogate state court complaint, summary judgment motion, trial brief, and closing statement in one document. Completeness, accuracy, reliability, and veracity will forestall most claim objections. False, wrong, incorrect, overstated, and fraudulent claims will land the claimant and attorney in a big world of hurt.

Preference Lawsuits and Other Claims

What is a preference? Bankruptcy Code Section 547(b) enables the trustee or debtor in possession (or successor) to recover payments made by the debtor to (a) its creditors, in payment of a (b) debt owed by the debtor to the creditor, if (c) paid within 90 days for the date of filing (d) on account of an antecedent debt, and (e) which enables the creditor to get more than other creditors. Included are liens, levies, enforcement, transfers to pay a debt, or security within 90 days. The trustee (or others) file a suit in bankruptcy court to recover these transfers.

What does antecedent debt mean? A debt that is past due.

The creditor has defenses to a preference action as follows: (1) the payments were made in the ordinary course of business or ordinary business terms, (2) the payments were an account of C.O.D. sales or contemporaneous transfers, (3) the creditor provided "new value" after receipt of the preferential transfers, (4) and the preference lawsuit must be brought within two years of the appointment of the trustee but before the case is dismissed or closed (Section 546(a) (1) &(2)).

A confirmed plan in a large case authorizes the trustee or third party designee to file preference law suits, which number in the hundreds or more. Some law firms have specialized in mass preference lawsuits. Preference lawsuits are a fact of life but detested by the business community because the creditor has done nothing wrong, insurance does not cover the claims, and the plaintiff sues where the bankruptcy was filed, which is typically Delaware or New York (SD NY), home to the major bankruptcies. Nearly all preference lawsuits are settled for a percentage on the dollar. Service of process of the lawsuit is by mail, which leads to an inordinate number of default judgments because the defendants fail to recognize that they have been sued for money damages.

The trustee can also sue to recover a fraudulent conveyance made by the debtor, set aside (vacate) liens that have not been perfected by the filing of a financing statement (UCC-1) with the secretary of state or the recording of a deed of trust with the recorder, and avoid statutory liens. The trustee can recover the property of the estate.

If the trustee recovers the preferential transfer (the claw back), the creditor can file a proof of claim based on the return of the preference. Expect only pennies on the dollar.

Notice of Hearing (or Motion) to Approve Disclosure Statement

Let's start with the rudiments first. Chapter 11 requires a debtor to file a disclosure statement, subject to court approval, and plan of reorganization (i.e., the "plan") upon which the creditors vote. Call this insolvency democracy. Call this a lot of paper. Consider a disclosure statement the first cousin to a security or debt prospectus filed with the Securities and Exchange Commission. The disclosure statement enables the creditor to make an insured decision to vote for, or against, the proposed plan of reorganization.

The disclosure statement provides the history of the debtor, why the debtor got into trouble, who is running the show, how the debtor is going to pay back creditors, whether this plan is feasible (the "show me the money" moment), the creditor entities, why the Chapter 11 is better than a Chapter

7, and the risks inherent in the plan. This is a grand survey. If the debtor is American Airlines, expect a 600 page disclosure statement. If the debtor is Bob's Hotdog Stand, expect a six page disclosure statement.

In large cases, creditors, the U.S. Trustee, or the creditor's committee might litigate the sufficiency of the disclosure statement. If the debtor has 10,000 creditors, which might include governments, large institutions, and taxing authorities, and proposes a multi-billion Chapter 11 plan, the details are important. Each of these details are irrelevant to some but relevant to others, which means that the disclosure statement rivals old time phone books.

In small to medium size cases, bankruptcy judges disdain petty fighting over disclosure statements because the debtor's business is well known to the creditors.

The value offered by disclosure statements is the explanation of what (or how much) creditors are receiving and why the plan is a better deal than a liquidation. Many Chapter 11s offer creditor's stock in the new entity that emerges from the Chapter 11. In a handful of cases, the revested entity is a corporation that lists its stock on the stock exchanges. For large institutional creditors, or major debt buyers, the disclosure statement explains why the debtor's plan is worthwhile, and therefore, why the creditor should vote for the plan.

Notice of Hearing on Confirmation of Chapter 13

First, what is Chapter 13? Chapter 13 is a plan that enables a debtor to pay creditors a percentage on the dollar (or nothing for that matter) over five years and in exchange receive a discharge. That sounds great. Pay nothing and get off the hook? That's right. Courts have confirmed zero payment to unsecured Chapter 13 plans. A debtor who owes more than $250,000 unsecured (and subject to increases) or $750,000 secured (and subject to increases) must file Chapter 11.

Why is Chapter 13 important? Under the 2005 changes to the Bankruptcy Code, any wage earner making more than the state median for income had to file Chapter 13. Next, and more important, the Chapter 13 is a super discharge, which means that the debtor gets off the hook of liabilities beyond the Chapter 7 discharge. The poster child is *United Student Aid Funds Inc. vs. Espinosa* (2010) 559 U.S. 260, which discharged student loans.

At the outset of the Chapter 13, the court sets two dates: first, the date to file objections to the proposed plan and, second, the date set for confirmation. These are dates that are certain. Be on time or be in default. The paperwork is not too intensive but very time sensitive. Each bankruptcy has their own rules. The FMC notice usually provides the drop dead dates.

To get a plan confirmed, the debtor must pay the creditors what they would get in a Chapter 7, but based on the debtor's disposable income (net wages). What the debtor makes, the expenses, other contingencies, and the liabilities can be contested. The upside is that most debtors, when faced with a bona fide plan objection, will file an amended plan and offer more money to the creditor. Sometimes, though rarely, the debtor digs in his or her heels and lets the judge decide how much he or she must pay.

The Chapter 13 trustee might object but rarely drives a case to a final hearing. Do not expect the Chapter 13 trustee to birddog every case.

The downside of Chapter 13 litigation is that the debtor is only paying pennies on the dollar. Should the creditor succeed in compelling the debtor to pay 25% on the dollar, as opposed to 15% on the dollar, the spread is only 10%, which is not much and rarely enough money to pay for the attorney's fees and expenses. These cases are also time consuming.

Notice of Hearing on Confirmation of Chapter 11

This is a two page treatment of a subject that can span 1,000 pages plus an index, table of contents, and pictures.

What is Chapter 11? Chapter 11 enables business (and individuals) to pay creditors what they would get in a Chapter 7 through a court ordered plan. The creditors trade out their claims and receive the benefits under the plan. In exchange, the debtor gets a discharge.

The parties to the case are the debtor (and attorneys in two), the creditor's committee (and attorneys), the secured creditors (and attorneys), the U.S. Trustee (if a very large case), and other third parties who might have an interest. Ten to 20 parties might have a viable interest in the case, but the major player is the committee and attorney.

The debtor can offer many things, including: (1) a payment program; (2) a one time payment of a percentage on the dollar or a "pot plan" (whatever money is in a pot); (3) an earn-out from future profits (net or gross), due from the debtor or the buyer of the debtor's assets; (4) stock in the debtor or the debtor's buyer; (5) non cash coupons for the purchase of product, merchandise, or even meals; (6) payment, if any, from the debtor lawsuits against a third party, recovery of preference payments, or other litigation. This list is endless.

Upon confirmation, the plan discharges the debts, imposes an injunction upon pre-petition creditors, and revests the assets in the hands of the debtor or a newly created entity. Many plans discharge a broad range of obligations, including guaranties held by creditors who are entitled to sue non debtor guarantors, or bar other litigation.

To confirm a plan, the debtor circulates a court approved disclosure statement. The creditors vote on the plan and, assuming the winning hand, the court will confirm the plan.

This is the good news. The bad news is that a huge percentage of cases never get to plan confirmation, and more cases collapse even after plan confirmation. (The academic debate of this issue in the law reviews includes Elizabeth Warren and Jay Lawrence Westbrook's "The Success of Chapter 11: A Challenge to the Critics," *Michigan Law Review* [Vol. 107:603] (2008). Professor Warren is now a U.S. senator from Massachusetts.)

Many cases are bad and some are super bad. Some debtors fail to pay debt during the case. These debts are called administrative debts, which must be paid in full and in cash as condition of plan confirmation. The debts also include the attorney's fees. The total necessary to confirm the plan is called the plan deposit.

The court sets a deadline for plan objections, which require the filing of the plan objection and service upon all interested parties. This is a date certain. However, even though a claimant filed a late objection, the court might hear the late objection or address the objection because the court has an independent duty to insure that the plan complies with Bankruptcy Code Section 1129. An objector should file any objection on time, and in strict conformity with the court's scheduling order, but a late filed objection might take a seat at the table.

Common confirmation tricks in Chapter 11 plans are that a creditor will only get paid if the creditor votes for the plan, or only if it offers its federal TIN number, or that some contingency might or might not occur which might preclude payment. A creditor (or attorney) needs to flyspeck the plan and the disclosure statement.

A plan is a court order that bears collateral estoppel and res judicata consequences. A plan is a contract between the debtor and the creditors that can be enforced in state court proceedings. A plan is a consent decree that might (maybe) subject the debtor to continuing jurisdiction.

A default in a plan invokes *Alice In Wonderland*. The focal point is the plan. What are the remedies, if any, available to creditors should the debtor default? This is a very big deal. Many plans lack effective remedies available to creditors, among others, in the event of default. The typical remedy is that the creditor would file a motion to convert the case to Chapter 7.

Some bankruptcy judges deny these motions if the plan is significantly consummated and relegate the creditor to their plan remedies (if any). In other cases, the plan might even lack a provision that insures continuing bankruptcy court jurisdiction, which even further hinders bankruptcy court relief. If the debtor defaults in making payment, the creditor could file suit in state court, but the creditor's damage consists of the dividend (what the creditor would get under the plan). If the payment due the creditor is 10 cents on the dollar, the state court litigation is not cost effective. Post confirmation, the creditor's committee is disbanded in most cases. The U.S. Trustee is not supervising the debtor.

Post plan confirmation, nobody is watching the store. Worse, the plan, which might offer payments to the creditors, is a de facto IOU note, which is generally unsecured. Should the debtor rack up, post petition, more debt and more liens, the plan obligations are subordinate to the post petition debt, which is code word for a total disaster.

Chapter 11 offers alternative endings. A debtor who is operating a viable, but financially doomed, business would file Chapter 11 and immediately move for the sale of the business. These are prepackaged sales, which the courts routinely approve. The debtor thereafter moves to convert to Chapter 7. The sale, and conversion to Chapter 7, is the de facto plan. These are called liquidating Chapter 11s. They are common, even though the purpose of Chapter 11 is for the debtor to prosecute a formal plan that would provide for payment of something to creditors. These liquidating Chapter 11s, which incorporate a sale order, might not provide anything to creditors.

Notice of Abandonment of Assets

The trustee can abandon an asset of the estate if the asset is valueless, burdensome, or subject to environmental burdens that hobble administration of the asset. In most (90% of these cases) the creditors do not care. In some, and very few cases, a creditor might care if the creditor perceives that the asset does have value or should be administered. The common scenario is that the trustee abandons real estate that in fact has substantial value.

In objecting to an abandonment, the creditor has to timely object, which means filing papers with the court and service by mail on those parties who do not receive electronic services of process.

Notice of Sale of Asset Free and Clear of Liens

Unlike state court proceedings, the trustee can sell the assets, free and clear of the liens that encumber the real property, in their pecking order, just like the order on a totem pole. The acid test is the trustee has to allege the lien is subject to a good faith dispute, which is not too onerous.

The trustee files the motion for a sale to bona fide buyer, consummates the sale, and impounds the proceeds pending a resolution of the lien claims. This is a common proceeding. Most creditors stipulate to this relief but demand that the trustee take prompt action to resolve the lien claims.

As with all bankruptcy motions, the creditor must timely file and serve an opposition.

Notice to File Reclamation Claims

Here is the primer. If a creditor sells on good credit within 20 days prior to the bankruptcy, but the goods are consumed (food service products, wholesale groceries, etc.), the creditor can file a priority claim under Bankruptcy Code Section 503(b)(9). If the goods still exist, post petition, the creditor can timely demand reclamation.

In large cases, the debtor faces thousands of these claims. Early in the case, the debtor seeks an order (which is always granted) that compels the reclamation creditors to file their claims with a claims administrator (or even the debtor) within a limited period of time. The claim administrator would either "accept" the claim, "reject" the claim, or specify what portion of the claim is allowable and what portion is subject to rejection. The creditor might agree to the debtor's analysis and end the matter. Most (90% plus) of reclamation claims are fairly resolved through this process. This regime is an expectation.

The linchpin is filing the claims on time, and insuring the claim package is complete.

Notice to File Administrative Claims (or Claims Arising from Rejection of Executory Contracts)

An executory contract is a contract in which the performance is evergreen. The parties continue to perform through periodic cycles. In English, executory contracts are personal and real property leases, IP licenses (copyrights and patents), franchise agreements, supply contracts, and other contracts in which performance is continuing. The most common is the real property lease for the business itself. In a Chapter 7, the trustee has 60 days to accept or reject. Chapter 11s do not have a specific time table, but the court will set an order that requires a creditor, holding a rejected contract, to timely file a proof of claim. In most large Chapter 11s, the debtor can reject the executory contract through the plan or before the plan.

Watch for the notice. Insure that you timely file, which is the major hurdle.

Notice of Closure of Case

The court sends out a notice of case closing. This notice means that the assets (if any) are liquidated, and the proceeds distributed, any litigation is ended, and nothing else is pending. The closure of the case lifts the automatic stay, which itself is replaced by the permanent injunction.

Non Dischargeability Claims: Getting Even or Wasting Money?

Aside from the curlicues of the super discharge in a Chapter 13, the discharge in a Chapter 7 will extinguish claims against the debtor for fraud, breach of fiduciary duty and defalcation, and willful and malicious conduct (Section 523(a)(2),(4) and (6)). Other exceptions to the discharge abound, but this threesome is the most important, because the creditor must file a lawsuit within 60 days from the date of the first meeting of creditors to prove that the claim meets the statutory criteria. *Willful* means that the debtor intended the consequences of the wrongful act, as opposed to negligence. *Maliciousness* means a subjective, not objective, state of mind, consisting of malice directed to the plaintiff. Double back on your own research given the disparities in these rulings.

In addition, if the debtor filed fraudulent schedules, lacks books and records to explain his (or her) financial condition, cannot account for assets, violates a court order, fails to appear at the first meeting of creditors, or commits a fraudulent conveyance within one year, the debtor might forfeit the discharge completely. The debtor would remain "on the hook" for the claims even though the debtor forked over the assets to the trustee to pay creditor's claims (Section 727(a)(2)-(7)). Again, the creditor, or trustee, must file suit within 60 days from the first meeting.

The rules are easy. If a person commits some heinous act, bankruptcy declines to launder out that claim, but only if the creditor sues to exempt the debt or bar the discharge. Let's parse out this process. First, the burden falls upon the creditor to hire (and pay for) an attorney, insure that the case is winnable, and drive the case to trial. Next, the creditor has to win. Winning is tough because the creditor has to prove the case from "snout to tail." If the creditor sued the debtor in state court, which resulted in a very detailed, fact driven judgment, the bankruptcy court will abide by the state court judgment. This is a called collateral estoppel, which would enable the creditor to win hands down. Absent the prior state court judgment, the attorney and creditors are going to huff, and puff, and blow your house down. These cases might accrues fees and costs that might exceed $10,000 (depending upon the part of the country) or much more.

And if the creditor wins? Congratulations! Can the creditor collect? Good question. The pre-petition assets belong to the trustee. The debtor is, shall we say, bankrupt. The debtor might or might not have significant post bankruptcy income. The debtor might have a modest job that pays a living wage. The creditor might never collect, no matter the harm perpetrated by the debtor. The creditor would have difficulty in retaining an attorney unless the creditor paid by the hour and offered a very large retainer to finance post judgment enforcement. The creditor faces throwing good money after bad, which includes already investing $10,000 or more just to win in bankruptcy court.

Bankruptcy offers the rancid cocktail of a fact driven, tough, and timely filed case, spending good money to insure the debt survives the discharge, and running smack dab into the fact that the debtor is "judgment proof." While undefined in the bankruptcy code, the creditor emerges from this process very "bent out of shape." It is bad that the debtor robbed the creditor. Worse, the debtor filed bankruptcy. Worst, the creditor spent more money to chase down the debtor, which culminates in a empty judgment.

Informal Notice Is Notice of Every Date, Including the Date to File a Proof of Claim and Date to File a Non Dischargeability Proceeding

The debtor must schedule the name and current address of the creditors to insure the creditor receives timely notice of the proceedings.

What happens when the debtor fails to schedule the creditors? Let's go through the scenarios:

A. No formal notice, but the debtor *timely* notifies the creditor (or attorney or agent). The operative word is "timely." Informal notice is deemed notice of all due dates, including the filing of a proof of claim, and the filing of the non dischargeability complaint. Typically, the debtor is anxious to tell everyone that the debtor filed bankruptcy in order to get "kick" off the various bar dates.

B. No formal notice, but debtor provides notice on the cusp of the bar dates. Imagine the debtor calling the creditor the day before the bar dates for the key events. Consistently, the court reject this stunt as a substitute notice mandated by the Bankruptcy Code.

C. No notice at all. This is a common problem. Somebody got missed. Here are the rules from *In re Beezley*, 994 F.2d 1433 (9th Cir. 1993) and its many offspring:

1. Even without notice, all claims are discharged, but see below. Notice to the creditors, one way or another, does not render a particular claim dischargeable or non dischargeable.

2. If the claim is consensual or based on negligence, and the case had no money, the claim is forever discharged, even though the creditor did not participate in the case itself. Call this outcome "no harm, no foul," because the debt was subject to discharge, and the creditor did not get a dividend. Many creditors find this outcome unfair because the debtor can exclude creditors from a proceeding as long as the creditor does not take a hit.

3. If the claim is potentially non dischargeable (fraud, breach of fiduciary duty, or willful and malicious conduct) and the creditor truly did not get notice, the debt is not discharged. However, this is the first half of the equation. The creditor (or debtor) seeks a judicial adjudication. Someone has to file a lawsuit. Bankruptcy Rule 4007(c) requires that the creditor file the lawsuit within 60 days of the FMC, but given the lack of notice, the creditor can file the lawsuit at any time in bankruptcy or even state court. The creditor has to prove the lack of actual notice, and that the debtor is non dischargeable. Before ambling down this path, read *Beezley,* its progeny, and the local treatment of this difficult subject. Double down on grilling the debtor to ferret out whether the debtor provided actual notice, and grilling, again, the witnesses who allegedly received notice. More than one creditor exits court with lots of mud on their face when a witness chirps that the debtor in fact advised of the bankruptcy, but the creditor expected "formal notice." Notice is notice as long as the notice is timely.

If the debtor failed to schedule the creditor, and the creditor did not receive timely notice of the bankruptcy, opening the case to "re-start" the discharge clock does not work. Keep in mind that the debt, if falling into the *Beezley* pigeonhole, is potentially free of the automatic stay, and subject to the state statute of limitations in the filing of suit or renewal of a judgment.

Do Not Let It Slip Through the (Mailbox) Cracks

Bankruptcy law allows service of process by mail of lawsuits and claim objections at the last known address or sometimes a banker's lock box. A defendant expects that a process server will serve the lawsuit. Personal service of a lawsuit is deeply engrained in the court system but not the bankruptcy court.

Bankruptcy Rule of Procedure 7004(b)(1) authorizes service of process of a lawsuit (adversary proceeding) or significant motion (contested proceeding) as follows:

> Upon an individual other than an infant or incompetent, *by mailing a copy of the summons and complaint* to the individual's dwelling house or usual place of abode or to the place where the individual regularly conducts a business or profession.

Rule 7004(b)(3) allows service by mail as follows:

> Upon a domestic or foreign corporation or upon a partnership or other unincorporated association, by mailing a copy of the summons and complaint to the attention of an officer, a managing or general agent, or to any other agent authorized by appointment or by law to receive service of process and, if the agent is one authorized by statute to receive service and the statute so requires, by also mailing a copy to the defendant.

Paramount is to inscribe on the envelope, and proof of service, "Attn: Mr. Charles Cheese, President, Cheese Co., Inc., 1001 Cheese Blvd., Cheesetown, USA."

Given the plethora of mail that a bankruptcy case churns out and the unfamiliarity with service of process by mail, many creditors fail to grasp the significance of a mailed lawsuit, motion to avoid lien, or objection to claim, or other process. Getting served by mail just doesn't jar some folks into action, even though the mailing is good service.

Depending upon the unique facts of each case, service of process upon the creditor's lock box address might constitute valid service, even though the owner and holder of the box is the creditor's bank. Most banks turn over these documents, such as bankruptcy notices, to the creditor, but the delay can be prejudicial or the mail can be misdirected.

Automatic Stay #1: Contempt

Upon the filing of the bankruptcy, the court enters an order for "relief," which imposes the automatic stay under Bankruptcy Code Section 362

("Stay"). The Stay is an actual court order, like any other court order, that enjoins any action to collect a debt, sue, foreclose, sell the debtor's property in satisfaction of a debt, or continue with litigation. Everything must come to a full dead stop, including contacting the court to bring proceedings to a halt. Even the debtor's own appeal comes to a halt.

The automatic stay stops family law enforcement proceedings for money and personal injury actions even though the defendant is fully insured. The automatic stay bars the creditor from terminating, without a court order, a supply contract, IP lease, executory contract, or lease.

A creditor who violates the stay is in contempt of court. This is bad because the creditor is liable for damages, and potentially attorney's fees. In the event of a violation of the automatic stay, the creditor must affirmatively restore the debtor to the "pre stay" position. The typical stay violation is the creditor failing to stop litigation in progress, sending out demand letters, or repossessing a vehicle or foreclosing on a real property. Trustees or debtors are entitled to bring an action against the creditor and the creditor's attorney. These are serious lawsuits. Nobody likes to see their name as a defendant in a big time damage action brought by an ambitious debtor's counsel who smells blood in the water. Aside from the risk of damages, automatic stay litigation generates significant attorney's fees.

The automatic stay protects only the debtor and generally estate property. If the debtor filed Chapter 13, the automatic stay protects the debtor's spouse from enforcement arising from a consumer debt. This is called the co-debtor stay. The automatic stay does prevent the creditor from proceedings against partners, guarantors, indemnitors, sureties, joint tortfeasors, or other third parties.

Automatic Stay # 2: The Bitter Pill to Swallow

This section covers *In re Schwartz*, and the obligation to unwind or power to reinstate *nunc pro tunc*.

Bankruptcy upsets settled expectations in a contract. When the debtor files bankruptcy, the debtor defaults on payment. If the debtor is the seller of product, the unsold product becomes an asset of the estate. If the creditor had security, but the lien was not perfected by the filing of a financing with the secretary of state or by the recording of a deed of trust, the trustee can avoid the lien, which renders the debt owed to the creditor unsecured and probably unpaid. For the ill prepared, bankruptcy could be tragic.

What happens if the debtor files bankruptcy, but the creditor proceeds with a lawsuit, lien, enforcement, or asset sale. The post stay action is the "dark side of the moon." Actions taken post stay are void even if the creditor lacked any knowledge. The creditor bears an affirmative obligation, under penalty of contempt, to unwind the post stay actions that would restore the debtor to the pre-action status. The key case is *In Re Schwartz* (1992) 954 F. 2nd. 569, which holds that post stay action is void, and not voidable. This case is worth reading.

A common scenario is that the creditor unknowingly prosecutes a lawsuit, obtaining judgments or liens that encumber the debtor's property. Years later, when the debtor sells or refinances the property, she learns of the lien. The debtor demands that the creditor release the lien or face contempt. Is the debtor right? The answer is "yes" because the suit, judgment, and lien are all void even though the creditor was truly ignorant of the bankruptcy and, worse, the debtor hid the bankruptcy from the creditor.

The creditor can ask the bankruptcy court to lift and annul the automatic stay, *nunc pro tunc*. The court considers many factors (*In re Lett*, 238 B.R. 167, 195 (Bankr. W.D.Mo.1999)):

> (1) if the creditor had actual or constructive knowledge of the bankruptcy filing and, therefore, of the stay; (2) if the debtor has acted in bad faith; (3) if there was equity in the property of the estate; (4) if the property was necessary for an effective reorganization; (5) if grounds for relief from the stay existed and a motion, if filed, would likely have been granted prior to the automatic stay violation; (6) if failure to grant retroactive relief would cause unnecessary expense to the creditor; and (7) if the creditor has detrimentally changed its position on the basis of the action taken.

The gate keeper issue is whether the creditor had actual or constructive notice of the bankruptcy. Assuming absolutely no notice, the next step is the egregiousness of the debtor in failing to advise the creditor. Once the court gets past these two gate keeper issues, the court might (or might not) grant relief. Had the creditor gotten notice, the creditor would have recovered nothing anyway. Annulling the automatic stay is a windfall based happenstance. On the other hand, if the creditor actively litigated a case up and down the courts in which the defendant (the debtor) said nothing and only sprang the bankruptcy at the last moment when the case was going south, the court might annul the automatic stay. PACER and public record research and reasonable diligence would unearth the bankruptcy. This body of law is well understood. The path to annulling the automatic stay is well trodden.

Annulling the automatic stay to revive a void judgment is a big deal. Bankruptcy judges are not pro-debtor or pro-creditor. Under the right facts and a good presentation, a court might revive a void lien, which might insure payment of the debt.

Special Rules for Personal Injury Claims

The automatic stay stops a personal injury lawsuit in its tracks even though the debtor has insurance. The plaintiff must seek relief from the automatic stay, which is routinely lifted if the insurance will adequately cover the risk. Even if the insurance is inadequate, the court will lift the stay, which permits the creditor to continue with the current personal injury action or file suit. If the amount of the judgment exceeds the insurance, the creditor can file a proof of claim in the estate. No matter what, absent a special court order, the automatic stay stops the prosecution of the case against the debtor.

Most mega cases cycle in and out of bankruptcy through a Chapter 11, which discharges the debtor of all pre-petition and even pre-confirmation claims. This discharge would wipe out not only contract but also tort claims. To put a human face on this problem, the victims of the faulty ignition switch in the GM case are seeking to trump this plan discharge in order to litigate their claims.

Personal injury attorneys should read everything coming out the bankruptcy court, including sale orders that might discharge potential successor liability against the buyer of the assets. In many cases, the buyer is not a new entity, but a newly reconstructed entity to warehouse key assets and leave the debris behind. See *In re Motors Liquidation Co.*, No. 09-50026 (REG), 2015 WL 1727285 (Bankr. S.D.N.Y. Apr. 15, 2015), which knocked out potential claims based on a sale order that barred successor liability. Vigilance is a necessity. Paranoia is justified.

What happens when the plaintiff files bankruptcy? Let's play hide and go seek. If the plaintiff files bankruptcy but does not schedule the personal claim (or case) as an asset, the defendant can seek to dismiss the case on the basis that the trustee owns the claim. The defendant can likewise seek to dismiss the case because the claim was not scheduled and therefore does not exist. Defendants have enjoyed great success in getting lender liability claims when the debtor has not scheduled nor listed them in the disclosure statement or plan of reorganization. Employment claims, including wage, hour, harassment, discrimination, etc., claims are subject to dismissal if undisclosed in the schedules and statement of affairs. More than one plaintiff who filed bankruptcy to discharge consumer debt but failed to disclose a multi-million dollar case or judgment has been confronted with a potential dismissal or a successful "grab" by the bankruptcy trustee.

If the debtor schedules the claim, and it shows some viability, the trustee can prosecute the case through special counsel. Defendants relish the plaintiff filing bankruptcy because the trustee is generally inclined to settle major litigation for the right price because rarely does the trustee have the financial resources to finance the litigation. More than one aggrieved defendant has daydreamed of tossing the plaintiff into an involuntary bankruptcy, which, if converted, would put the claim in the hands of a pliable trustee. Nearly all of these schemes die on the vine.

The first moral of this tale is to always check, and re check, whether any of the parties have filed bankruptcy, including the plaintiff. The filing of a bankruptcy would appear on a public records search offered by Westlaw, Lexis-Nexus, or Dunn & Bradstreet. A public records search reaches only public information (as opposed to retrieving someone's credit report, which would invoke the federal and state Fair Credit Reporting Act and the federal and state Fair Debt Collection Practices Act).

The second moral is the plan specific machinery. Most mega bankruptcies are Chapter 11s that succeed in producing a plan of reorganization. Some plans require the tort claimants to file their claims with a special administrator on before a very specific date. Asbestos victims' plans create a trust fund that allows pre and petition claimants to timely file claims or else be barred. These trust funds consist of insurance proceeds, corporate stock of the revested entity, and post plan profits from the revested entity. (By the way, the fancy word for what the the asbestos trust funds do is "channeling the claims" away from the debtor and into the trust. Repeat this at a cocktail party, and your friends might believe that you are a bankruptcy maven.) PI attorneys must read the plan, which is a judgment, contract, and consent decree that might impair, alter, or reroute the PI case.

Serial Bankruptcies

When an individual or business files bankruptcy, it faces great hurdles in timely filing schedules, a statement of affairs, sworn compliance with credit counseling, and other "life or death" filings. Without nailing down specifics, some Chapter 11s and 13s are dismissed at the outset based on the failure to timely file court ordered documents. This is called an "administrative dismissal." These administrative dismissals are done in secret, unless the creditor has filed a request for special notice to keep apprised of the proceedings. Absent receipt of the dismissal, the creditor might proceed down the path of blissful ignorance while awaiting some actual notice from the court because the creditor's claim was never listed.

Without a rarely encountered bar to refiling, the debtor can refile, but must seek an order that would extend the stay beyond the first 30 days.

Serial filings are the bane of the bankruptcy court because the debtor, through these filings, tries to fend off the residential foreclosure. Worse for the creditors is the requirement to file new proofs of claims, and moreover request for special notice.

The Illusion of Chapter 13

Chapter 13 enables the wage earner to pay his (or her) obligations over a span of three to five years in exchange for the super discharge. Chapter 13s are well understood, well managed by the courts, and easy to understand. The legal community offers many experienced and hardworking Chapter 13 attorneys. This is the good news.

The bad news is that Chapter 13 does not work. Here are Judge Wayne Johnson's statistics from his "Standing Order Regarding Procedures for Chapter 13 Cases Assigned to Judge Johnson" (available online):

As a statistical matter, Chapter 13 cases fail considerably more often than they succeed. Nationwide, only one-third of Chapter 13 cases succeed. Only one in three debtors nationwide actually makes all the required plan payments which means two-thirds (67%) of Chapter 13 cases fail nationwide . . .

In the Central District of California, however, the data is even worse. A review of the Court's records a few years ago indicated that only 3% of Chapter 13 cases in this district resulted in a completed plan with Chapter 13 debtors making all plan payments. In 97% of Chapter 13 cases, debtors fail to make all payments required under their proposed plans.

In this division—Riverside Division,—the failure rate is not quite 97%, but still far above the national average of 67%. The Chapter 13 standing trustee in this division has calculated that 92% of all Chapter 13 cases fail . . .

According to the Court's own records, approximately 44% of all Chapter 13 cases in this division of this district are filed by debtors who lack counsel and nearly 100% of these cases fail. Debtors who file the other 56% of Chapter 13 cases are represented by counsel, but those cases fail at the rate of approximately 86%. This means that only 14% of Chapter 13 cases involving attorneys succeed and virtually 0% of Chapter 13 cases filed by unrepresented debtors succeed. Thus, while nationwide about two-thirds (67%) of all Chapter 13 cases fail, the failure rate in this division is twenty-five percentage points higher at 92%. In other words, the success rate of Chapter 13 cases nationwide (33%) is four times higher than in this division (8%).

Chapter 13 sometimes offers illusory promises. Is this really important? Yes, this is important because creditors should remain alert to the dismissal of the first case and refile in the second case, which the debtor is certain to file. Attorneys should advise that a Chapter 13 might be a clunker. Mind you, some Chapter 13s are barn burners. Some debtors pay 100% on the dollar. Given the historic low success rates, however, the creditor should have low (or no) expectations of payment.

Plans Are Confirmed Even if They Are Wrong

The bankruptcy court can confirm an plan even though the plan contains provisions that contravene the bankruptcy code. In *Levy vs. Cohen* (1977) 19 Cal. 3rd. 165, the California State Supreme Court upheld the dismissal of a general partner from state court litigation because the Chapter 11 plan for the partnership discharged the partner's liability for the debts. The creditors did not object to the plan. Bankruptcy Act (prior Section 5j) barred discharge of general partners in a general partnership bankruptcy. The creditor did not object to the discharge provision in the plan.

In addition to this state law case, some confirmed Chapter 11s discharge the liability of a guaranty (i.e., a non debtor) owed to a creditor in a case. Here are the typical facts:

> *Iberiabank did not attend the confirmation hearing or object to the Plan.* On March 21, 2011, the bankruptcy court entered an order confirming the Plan. No party appealed the confirmation order.

> In July 2012, Iberiabank commenced collection efforts in state court against the Loan's six individual guarantors, including Mr. Geisen, because a deficiency remained when the collateral securing the Loan was sold. Mr. Geisen responded that the Plan released him from his personal guaranty of the Loan. On March 29,

2013, Iberiabank reopened the bankruptcy case and moved for a determination that its claims against Mr. Geisen were not released. After a hearing, the bankruptcy court denied Iberiabank's motion. The bankruptcy court held that "every creditor of FFS was, in effect, giving a general release to Bradford Geisen, who is the debtor's principal." [citation omitted] Sitting as an appellate court, the district court affirmed the bankruptcy court's decision. Iberiabank now appeals to this Court.

> *In re FFS Data, Inc.,* 776 F.3d 1299, 1303 (11th Cir. 2015) [emphasis added]

A confirmation order incorporates the plan of reorganization, which becomes a judgment of the bankruptcy court as follows:

> A bankruptcy court's confirmation order that is final and no longer subject to appeal becomes "res judicata to the parties and those in privity with them." *Travelers Indemnity Co. v. Bailey,* 557 U.S. 137, 152, 129 S.Ct. 2195, 174 L.Ed.2d 99 (2009) (quotation omitted); [citation omitted]. Confirmation orders that satisfy the requirements for res judicata are given preclusive effect. [citation omitted] A reorganization plan that is incorporated into a confirmation order has the same res judicata effect.

See id. at 1300. *In re FFS Data, Inc.,* 776 F.3d 1299, 1306 (11th Cir. 2015)

United Student Aid Funds Inc. vs. Espinosa (2010) 559 U.S. 260 discharged student loans because the student loan servicer failed to object. A debtor can only seek a discharge of student loans based on hardship, which requires notice and hearing (11 U.S.C.A. §§ 523(a)(8) and 1328(a)(2)). The creditor did not object to the Chapter 13 plan.

The consistent theme is these cases that the attorney for the creditor did not object to the plan. Clearly this was an error—and, worse, an inexplicable error. Chapter 11 and Chapter 13 plans are written by attorneys for the debtor who insert provisions that favor the debtor (and its principals) to the detriment of the creditors. While the case law imposes fiduciary duties upon the Chapter 11 debtor, those duties evaporate when the debtor prosecutes a hidden agenda rife with releases of personal guaranties and injunctions against third party litigation, including potential regulatory, antitrust, or other third party claims. Other preclusive orders are orders approving the sale of assets under Bankruptcy Code Section 363, which bars successor liability. For example, as mentioned above, economic claims from GM's faulty ignition switches were barred from successor liability against the New GM because the sale order precluded these suits (*In re Motors Liquidation Co.,* No. 09-50026 (REG), 2015 WL 1727285 (Bankr. S.D.N.Y. Apr. 15, 2015)).

While the bankruptcy judge might (or might not) take issue with a pro-hibited term which might prompt the denial of a Chapter 11 or Chapter 13 plan confirmation, the creditor is obligated to object. Speak or forever hold your peace. When in doubt, object; even a one page objection, in a pinch, might be sufficient.

In the next chapter, we move from the structured, judicially supervised realm of bankruptcy to the murkier land of assignment for the benefit of creditors.

10
Assignment for the Benefit of Creditors

The Short Story

Synopsis

An assignment for the benefit of creditors enables a distressed business the opportunity to liquidate its assets, pay secured creditors and taxes, and distribute the proceeds, if any, to the creditors. Assignments are very old, but superseded by bankruptcy given that bankruptcy offers the automatic stay, court supervision, subpoena powers, a specialized forum with a judge who can render a money judgment, and greater transparency.

In an assignment, the debtor voluntarily transfers its assets to a neutral third party with the directions to liquidate the assets; pay secured, administrative and priority creditors; and distribute the remaining funds to the unsecured creditors. Depending on the state, an assignment is private; it is not a judicial proceeding and it lacks any judicial supervision.

Legal Basis

Common law and statutory law, depending upon the state. Most assignment law arises from the law of contracts and trusts.

When Do I File a Claim?

The dates are established by the Assignee for the Benefit of Creditors (ABC), which can range from 30 to 90 days, unless set by state statute. The assignee sends out a notice with a due date, but prudence dictates filing a claim as soon as possible.

What Does It Mean to File a Claim?

Use personal delivery, overnight services, USPS Express mail, and maybe fax. Get proof of receipt. Email is unlikely, but don't hesitate to try. Getting the claim filed on time is important.

How Do I Locate the Filing?

This is very difficult. The assignee, or maybe the debtor, might send out notice, but notice might go to bank lock boxes or old addresses. You have to call. Be insistent. Assignment are not public filings. Don't expect notice from a public venue.

What Do I File?

The ABC might demand that you use its form of proof of claim, which closely resembles the forms used in bankruptcy court. Be very thorough in calculating the amount, which would include the principal, interest, attorney's fees, and court costs. Attach everything. Support the claim in great detail and support any claim of security, including a security interest, mortgage or deed of trust, or other.

Do I Get Accruing Interest?

Yes, for secured claims. Yes, for unsecured claims if the estate is solvent. No, for unsecured claims if the estate is insolvent.

Do I Need to Update the Claim?

Yes. It is a common error to presume that the assignee will ask for updates or that the assignee will calculate interest if the estate is fully solvent.

Who Gets the Claim?

The assignee, but prudence dictates sending the proof of claim to the assignee's attorney.

What Should I Include?

Everything. Leave nothing out. Thoroughness now will prevent you from attempting to locate paper documents a year later.

Are There Privacy Issues?

Redact social security numbers, driver's license numbers, bank account numbers, and other clearly private information. Delete any personal information.

What Should I Expect from the Assignee (and When)?

You might or might not receive an acknowledgment at all unless you provide a self addressed, stamped envelope or deliver the claim through a courier or counter service. Confirm receipt. It is a common error to assume without cause that the assignee actually got the claim.

Is There Judicial Supervision?

No, unless state enacted. Counsel should advise the client that the assignment lacks any judicial supervision. If the client has inside knowledge that the assignment is rife with fraud or that before the assignment the debtor spun off valuable assets, the client might want to consider filing an involuntary bankruptcy petition, assuming there are two other creditors.

Is There a Risk of Side Deals?

Yes, a very high one. Bankruptcies mandate disclosure of the current financial condition and, through the questions in the statement of affairs, some limited historical dates (i.e., transactions that took place in the past). Under Bankruptcy Rule 2004, the trustee or nearly anyone else (i.e., a creditor) may examine the debtor and seek the production of historical documents. Many creditors have a long history with the debtor that enables the debtor to pinpoint where the "bodies are buried." Some creditors warehouse major troves of financial disclosures. On the other hand, an assignment does not empower a creditor to examine the debtor. The ABC might or might not examine the debtor under oath. Common law does not mandate this right of an examination. Unless prompted by the creditors, few assignees engage in an forensic asset investigation.

Given these few, if any tools, that compel disclosure or an investigation, many debtors engage in massive asset reallocation (fancy word for skimming off key assets which go to insiders), looting of accounts, destruction or scrambling of records, or corporate reorganizations that shift assets out of the company. Side deals, pre-arranged insider transfers, diverting key assets, stealing AR checks as they arrive, and jumbling the records beyond comprehension are very common. Too frequently, assignments are a haven for side deals, theft, and embezzlements, which are swept under the table.

The real issue in assignments is disclosure of prior transactions. Bankruptcy compels the debtor to disclose prior transactions in the schedules and statement of affairs. With this paperwork as a roadmap, the bankruptcy trustee, U.S. trustee, or the creditors can investigate the prior transfers and, if appropriate, take action to unwind the transfers. An assignment does not provide for "look back" disclosures. Creditors do not have any mechanism to unearth prior transfers, liens, or conveyances. The assignee will be less than interested because nearly all transfers are to insiders or their families. An assignee who chases down these insider transactions might succeed in the case—however, given that the debtor's attorney has counseled the debtor to make an assignment, should the assignee sue the corporate insider or debtor (who followed the attorney's advice), the debtor's counsel would never (and never is really *never*) advise of a future assignment.

Are There Statutory Safeguards against Fraud?

None unless mandated by local law. Remedies, if any, are found in state court; they are few and far between given the lack of disclosure, the fact of costs, and the rarity of these proceedings.

Can Another Party Object to My Claim?

Yes and no. "Yes" because another creditor has standing, but "no" because the assignee has no clear duty to respond to another party's objection, but should make an investigation before payment of the claim. This is unlikely because assignments bear poor transparency. Creditors have limited knowledge of what claims have been filed and by whom.

If There Is an Objection, What Happens?

Depending upon the state, you might have to file suit and seek an injunction against the assignee from distributing money to the other creditors. This will be an expensive process because the objection is not a simple filing but a full fledged state court lawsuit.

What Does the ABC Provide at Close?

Most assignees provide a closing letter, which generally describes the assets and liabilities. Other assignees provide a detailed accounting and even a list of creditors. Few assignees provide an accounting and an opportunity to object. Accountings range from something close to bankruptcy proceedings to . . . not so much. Assignees are generally subject to trust law that mandates an accounting but not necessarily specific details.

What Are the Priorities?

Taxes, wages, escrow and attorney fees, secured claims, PACA claims, statutory priorities, labor claims, landlords' claims (maybe), U.S. government claims, claims of property owners, and—finally—unsecured creditors. More important, priority is given by the ABC to anyone else at the ABC's discretion.

Do I Have an Obligation to Object to Another Claim?

Generally this is a hollow right because creditors are rarely given a list of other creditors, copies of their claims, or the basis of the claims. Insiders, wage claimants, and third parties can file all sorts of bogus but seemingly regular claims, and nobody would have notice or an opportunity to object. Insiders can masquerade as unpaid wage claimants. Insiders can file claims of unpaid loans that are nonexistent, falsified, paid in part or in whole, or are disguised capital. Assignees are not receptive to internecine battles, particularly if the targets are the corporate principals who executed the assignment in the first place.

When Can I Object?

Maybe never, if you do not have notice.

Do I Have Remedies if a Bad Claim Has Been Filed?

File suit against the assignee if you have timely notice. Be prepared to post a bond if the court grants an injunction. Should you lose the suit for one reason or another, you might be liable for costs and fees based on the bond or damages recoverable under the injunction. Moreover, if your objection is deemed unfounded or totally meritless, as the case might be, you might find yourself subject to the attorney's fees incurred by the assignee in responding to the lawsuit. Some assignees might respond by filing an interpleader which would accrue significant expense and fees, all paid from the top and in favor of the attorney for ABC.

What About Accuracy of Claims and Liability?

Absent specific state law that deals with Assignment for the Benefit of Creditors, filing a bad claim is only subject to general state court remedies for fraud.

Is Compliance with FDCPA Required?

Probably. This includes an entire body of federal and state consumer protection law.

When Do I See an Accounting or Money?

At close of the case, which might span years. Assignments tend to run one to two years or more. Accounting might range from a final letter that generally describes the estate and encloses a check or a detailed "line by line accounting" of receipts and disbursements along with a check (or as the case might be, no check). Assignees are not required to provide a detailed accounting, which raises issues about the reasonableness of attorney fees and charges, assignee's fees and charges, and the costs of administration.

When Should I Expect Payment?

In 12 to 36 months or more.

How Is Transparency?

Good, fair, poor, or terrible, depending upon the assignee.

What Are Some Other Options?

An involuntary bankruptcy, if possible. The bankruptcy court might abstain given an ongoing assignment for the benefit of creditors.

Stay of Legal Proceedings?

No, but suing the debtor (the assignor) is futile because the debtor transferred its assets to the assignee. The guarantor is fair game and should be pursued.

Guarantor Status?

Depending upon the guaranty, the failure to file a claim in the assignment might exonerate the guarantor based on the failure of the creditor to act diligently. Filing a claim with the assignee is paramount.

Overall Fairness?

Good to poor—and sometimes awful. This strictly depends upon the honesty of the debtor, the efficiency and zeal of the assignee, whether insiders refrain from robbing everyone, and whether the case is relatively free of fraud and corruption.

ABCs are not a bargain. In one slip opinion, the court held that $35,000.00 as the *minimum* ABC fee was not justified, necessary, or reasonable in light of the charges of $7,978.30 for an inside employee. The court disallowed $1,026.94 for labor costs to scan documents (no invoice attached), $816.53 for allocation of costs for cell phone service among various unrelated general assignments administered . . . and $8,200 to a vendor of pre-petition IT services (*In re O'Reilly & Danko* 2013 WL 4548260, Slip Copy (USBC, 2013)). Given these prices and billing practices, ABCs are nearly as costly, or even more, than bankruptcy, in which the judges assiduously scrutinize professional fees and costs.

Depending upon the state, the ABC does have the power to recover fraudulent conveyances and even claw back preferential transfers analogous to bankruptcy preferences. Under certain circumstances, the assignee assumes the status of a lien creditor and might trump the rights of unsecured creditors under Article 9 of the UCC.

Right to Declare an Exemption?

Maybe, but maybe not—depends on state law. Few individuals would have proceeded with an assignment, so this question is moot.

Right of Reclamation?

UCC Code Section 2702 permits a creditor to reclaim goods sold within 10 days if the debtor is insolvent and further back based on a false financial statement. The reclamation rights of the creditor survive the assignment, which means that the assignee must return the goods to the creditor upon timely demand.

However, a debtor is inclined to "load up" on last minute credit sales, which are quickly resold for cash or incorporated into other products that are resold for cash. Cash proceeds exit the back door or pay for taxes or personal guaranteed debt that would burden the insiders. Unlike bankruptcy, if the goods are resold, the creditor rights vanish. Last minute credit purchases, which open up a subterranean cash flow, are "free money."

What Are My Proactive Strategies?

Depending on the state, an assignment might claw back liens, levies, attachments, and payments on an antecedent debt within 90 days; avoid unperfected liens; or recover fraudulent conveyances. For states without a claw back, a creditor is free to enforce the debt or judgment up to the last day. The reason is easy to see. An assignment only passes what the debtor owed as of the date of the assignment. If, for example, a creditor encumbered all assets the second before the assignment, the assignee is also subject to the creditor's lien.

An assignee is not a bona fide purchaser for value. Under the Uniform Commercial Code, an assignee is a lien creditor that might take priority over an unperfected security interest (i.e., a security interest in which the creditor failed to file a financing statement with the correct secretary of state). Some states might, or might not have, claw-back rights (i.e., the state version of a bankruptcy preference), which means, absent a claw-back right, the creditor can lien and levy up to the last date. An assignee might constitute a creditor for purpose of prosecuting a fraudulent conveyance action.

The Long Story

What Is an Assignment for the Benefit of Creditors (ABC)?

An ABC permits a financially troubled debtor the opportunity to turn over assets to a neutral person who would liquidate the assets and pay creditors. Sounds like a bankruptcy, so what is the difference? Good question.

Assignments are a really old legal concept. Assignments drift from the mists of English common law into American case law in the early 19th century (or maybe earlier). Among the legion of cases that uphold assignments are *Brainard vs. Fitzgerald* (1935) 3 Cal. 2nd. 157, which upheld a non statutory assignment for the benefit of creditors. See also *Bumb v. Bennett* (1958) 51 Cal. 2d 294, 333 P.2d 23 (1958), which repeats the message. The message from these California supreme court cases is "If it isn't broken, don't 'fix' it."

Is the Assignee the Agent for the Debtor? Or is the Assignee the Trustee for the Creditors?

An insolvent debtor hires an assignee to take possession of the debtor's assets, liquidate the assets, and pay creditors pro rata.

This sentence explains the universe of assignment. Let's parse it. Under a "general assignment," the debtor engages an assignee to liquidate its assets and distribute the proceeds to creditors. In accepting the general assignment, unfettered by the debtor's instructions, the assignee bears the trust responsibilities in favor of the creditors. The general assignment endows the assignee with the legal and beneficial title of the debtor's property. Most general assignments authorize the assignee to exercise its own discretion in the liquidation of the assets, the management of the estate, filing suit against third parties, hiring of professionals, and paying of creditors' claims.

Few assignments repose residual rights of the debtor to control the assignee. The most common right held by the debtor is to condition payment due a creditor if the creditor will release any rights to proceed against a third party surety (bonding company), joint tortfeasors, or guarantors. The fact that the fact that the debtor retains control abrogates the independence of the assignee, and might even render the fund in the hands of the assignee as the property of the debtor given the debtor's right of control. More than one creditor has levied on the assignee to reach estate funds on the basis that the debtor is still owner of the funds (based on the residual right of control, if any).

At the point of the assignment, the assignee becomes the trustee for the benefit of the creditors because the assignee holds the debtor's former property (and its ensuing proceedings) for purpose of payment of their claims. After liquidation and payment of administrative creditors, the assignee pays the creditors—after payment, of course, of senior claims and liens.

Why Bother with Assignment?

Why bother investing energy in ABCs when the U.S. Constitution guarantees bankruptcy? Article III offers jurisdiction for bankruptcy cases but refers nearly all matters to the U.S. Bankruptcy Court. Title 11 provides specialized bankruptcy judges, U.S. Trustees, and Chapter 7 and 13 trustees. The published cases originating from the bankruptcy judges (the trial bench) to the United States Supreme Court is first rate scholarship. Other than the filing fees, the U.S. government offers this vast judiciary for virtually no fee.

The Bankruptcy Code discharges unsecured debts, stays or restrains collection, sells assets free and clear of liens, discharges the debtors and might discharge a guarantor's liability (under a plan), stays a co-debtor liability in a Chapter 13, lien strips, and preserves exemption rights in exchange for debtor's sworn disclosures throughout the case. Schedules, statement of affairs, Rule 2004 examinations, and testimony at the first meeting of creditors or other examinations require sworn statements.

On the other hand, depending on state law, an assignment does not discharge debts nor compel disclosures. State law does not compel any sworn disclosures of the current or prior history of the debtor.

The fact that the debtor chooses to liquidate itself through an assignment, as opposed to a bankruptcy, suggests that the debtor might be hiding assets, pre-assignment conveyances, liens, and other transfers, and wishes to avoid disclosure through bankruptcy. These conveyances might include the fact that the insiders altered the accounting records to "write off" a debt owed by the insiders to the assignor (i.e., the debtor).

Who, or What, Are the Assignees?

Many bankruptcy trustees, professional receivers, insolvency attorneys, and professional liquidators will accept assignments. Many credit manager associations, wholesaler associations, and trade associations, including credit manager associations (Los Angeles) engage in robust assignment practices. These are called "adjustment houses." Wholesaler associations date back to the 19th century or earlier.

Key Similarities and Differences between Bankruptcy and Assignment

The Assets of the Debtor

When the debtor files bankruptcy, the trustee assumes legal title to the assets of the debtor. The trustee must liquidate (or abandon, if worthless) the assets and pay creditors. When the debtor assigns assets to the assignee for the benefit of creditors, the assignee assumes the identical task but is limited to the assignment, which might limit the scope of the assets or what assets the debtor reveals. If the debtor has previously conveyed assets, fraudulently or otherwise, the assignee does not take possession or title of them unless the assignee takes legal action to recover these assets. These fraudulent conveyance cases are valid unless the assignee succeeds in recovering the property.

What Prompts an Assignment as Opposed to a Bankruptcy Proceeding

The insider of the corporate debtor makes a decision whether to file a bankruptcy petition for the debtor entity or execute an assignment for the benefit of creditors. Rarely would the insider recover the net surplus from any insolvency proceedings. Administrative costs, taxes, wages, and creditors gobble up every nickel. Let's dig deeper.

Some liabilities are borne by the debtor and the insider. The liabilities include the bank line of credit, major leases (real and personal properties), unpaid payroll taxes, some tort claims, and trade vendor claims, if guaranteed. The insider might execute an assignment with an eye to paying claims that bear personal liability and with the support of, or even the direction of, the creditor holding a personal guaranty. A very clever insider might even grant a security interest in favor of the personal guaranty creditor to insure prompt payment.

On the other hand, an aggressive vendor (without a personal guaranty) might levy upon all the debtor's assets. The insider faces personal liability, say, to the IRS and to vendors, leasing companies, and third parties. Assuming that the state does not void a preference akin to Bankruptcy Code Section 547(b), the insider dumps the debtor into a Chapter 7 to unwind the levy, which would recover the assets for the benefit of a bankruptcy estate. Creditors would enjoy some distribution as opposed to none.

The insider often chooses a bankruptcy or an assignment in pursuit of a strategy that pays creditors who hold the insider personally liable.

The Liabilities of the Debtor

In both a bankruptcy and an ABC, taxes, wages, priority claims, costs of administration, and secured claims are paid first. Creditors get the crumbs. If the debtor in the bankruptcy is an individual, the debtor gets a discharge of the debt, save and except certain statutory exceptions.

In an ABC, absent an agreement by and among the creditors and the debtor (if an individual), the debt is not discharged. If the debtor is a corporation or LLC, the discharge is not important because the entity empties out its assets.

Commercial creditors, landlords, financial institutions, leasing companies, among others, demand a personal guaranty from the principal as a condition of the credit. Like a bankruptcy, the stay imposed by Bankruptcy Code Section 362, or discharge of the debts under Bankruptcy Code Section 727, does not discharge the guarantor's liability to the creditor. How can the guarantor, who is the insider to the debtor, exit those pesky, but life threatening personal guaranties? Technically the discharge is called guarantor Nirvana.

The answer is that the guarantor gins up a bunch of money—say, $100,000.00. The guarantor demands that the assignee offer the creditors holding a guaranty (i.e., a priority class of creditors) the sum of $100,000 as an added distribution to the guaranty creditors, which in addition to distribution due the creditors from the assets, the debtor due all creditors.

How is this offer made? Glad you asked. The guarantor deposits the $100,000.00, which the assignee divides pro rata among the guaranty creditors, less the assignee's charges, fees, and expenses. In making the final distribution to the guaranty creditors, the creditor attaches a letter that states that the guarantor offers the "added distribution," in exchange for a release under the guaranty. The back of the distribution check bears legend "Full settlement satisfaction of the claims of the payee against ABC Company and John Dole, Guarantor to the Payee." The letter also informs the creditors that funds due a non consenting creditor go back to the guarantor.

A bird in hand is worth two in the bush. Many creditors readily cash the check given that they wish to avoid accruing third party charges to litigate the guaranty. This stunt might wipe out all personal guaranties; anecdotal evidence suggests a 75% success rate. Believe it or not, this is a common practice.

Court Supervision

Depending on the state, the courts do not supervise an ABC. An ABC can set its own fees and charges, distribute the funds per the terms of the assignment contract, and might even demand a release from the creditors or compel the creditors to release their claims against the guarantors. The fact that the debtor seeks to control the assignee is evidence that the assignee is the debtor's agent, and for that matter, the funds held by the assignee are truly held for the benefit of the debtor and not the creditors.

Before going down the path that assumes the assignee is the wild and wily gunslinger in town, check local law to see if the legislature has installed the local marshal, better known as the court.

On the other hand, trustees operate under the auspices of the bankruptcy court, which must approve sales, fee applications, settlements, compromises, and just about any other major undertaking by the trustee. The court must approve a final accounting.

Liens Encumbering the Debtor's Assets

Generally, an assignee cannot avoid a creditor's liens. The assignee stands in the shoes of the assignor, which means that the assignee sells assets subject to the liens, which must be paid as a condition of the sale. If the property is over-encumbered, the assignee would be very hard pressed to sell the property given the lack of equity. In most cases, the assignee would abandon the property to the secured creditors.

The exception to the sanctity of creditor liens is that the assignee can avoid a lien if the lien was perfected within 90 days of the assignment. This right to avoid is analogous to a bankruptcy preference if allowed by statute. If the lien is fraudulent or unperfected, the assignee has the rights of a creditor under the Uniform Voidable Transactions Act and a lien creditor under Article 9 of the UCC.

If the creditor obtained a writ of attachment (a pre-judgment remedy), the fact of the assignment, depending upon state law, might avoid the attachment. Assuming a valid lien, the assignee sells the asset subject to the lien, or the debt secured by the lien is liquidated in the escrow, like any other sale.

Bankruptcy is a different kettle of fish, some of which are endangered. Bankruptcy Code Section 363(f) permits the trustee to sell assets free and clear of liens if the lien is in "bona fide dispute." Without breaking a sweat, most liens are in bona fide dispute.

Stays against Prosecution of Creditors' Claims

The filing of a bankruptcy invokes an automatic stay (i.e., a court order) that bars collection of any debt, enforcement of a judgment, foreclosure of real or personal property, or enforcement of any lien or levy. This is automatic, which means that the stay takes effect upon the filing of the bankruptcy. Every act, taken post petition, is void as a matter of law. A creditor faces contempt and damages if it violates the stay—even punitive damages. A creditor is liable for the attorney's fees to restore the debtor to the prepetition status.

On the other hand, absent some curlicue under state law, an assignment does not invoke any stay. A creditor is free to proceed against the debtor, post assignment. However, there is a big catch. Upon a valid assignment, the debtor transfers all assets to the assignee, who is the owner and holder of the assets for the benefit of the creditors. While the creditor might not violate a court order, analogous to a bankruptcy, the creditor would not reach any assets of the debtor, which are now in the possession of the assignee.

Some assignees are more clever than others. When a debtor reaches the nadir of this financial condition, the debtor consults with attorneys, liquidators, and sometimes professional assignees or adjustment agencies. The debtor complains that the creditors are filing lawsuits, levying bank accounts, seizing physical assets, or dragging insiders into court for near daily grilling. Some debtors complain that the creditor's attorneys are "dismembering the debtor." At the suggestion of its own attorney, the debtor grants the adjustment house a perfected security interest on behalf of all creditors. This is a total fraud.

First, the adjustment house (which is a glorified collection agency) is not the agent for the creditors. In fact, the adjustment house is the agent for the debtor. Next, the creditors did not agree to anything. A security interest is valid if supported by consideration that would support a simple contract. This security interest seeks to fends off a creditor's levy based on the apparent priority of the security interest in the debtor's assets. Many judgment creditors abandon enforcement in the face of the security interest given the expense and effort required to topple the fraudulent security interest.

An assignment will not stop a bona fide secured creditor. A secured creditor may foreclose on its collateral even in the hands of the assignee. A creditor who has properly levied and liened property prior to the assignment can continue to prosecute enforcement even though the debtor undertook an assignment for benefit of creditors.

Fees and Charges Due the Estate Administrator and Estate Professionals

In bankruptcy, the court authorizes the costs and fees due professionals down to the cent. Trustees' fees are set by statute. In fact, the court bears an affirmative duty to approve all professional fees. Sit a day or two in bankruptcy court. You will watch the judge eviscerate attorneys—from the bottom feeders to the Harvard blue bloods—for shoddy billing, wasted efforts, billing for clerical tasks, or, worse, see the judge deny fees for ethical violations. You'd think an old style barber pole flanked the bench. Why? The judge gives fee haircuts every day of the week.

In an assignment, the assignee can unilaterally decide what fees are to be paid and at what rate. The debtor and the assignee contractually set fees, which range from 5% to up to 33.3%, plus costs of administration. Costs including mailings, secretarial and administrative charges, third party professionals, "set-up fees," and other charges that might or might not pass bankruptcy muster. The creditors have little input other than claiming that the assignees' fees are unconscionable. Assignees will pay their own attorneys; the accountants; attorneys for a creditor's committee, if one is appointed; and maybe the attorney for the debtor. Most assignees attempt to pay what would appear to be reasonable fees. Sound okay? Not always. Reasonable people have different opinions, which means that the assignee typically pays the attorney's fees as tendered without much push back.

Sometimes, assignees seek compensation based on the accrual interest of funds held in trust. For example, an assignee sells an asset and collects the cash. Selling assets, appointing accountants to file tax returns, objecting or resolving claims, and otherwise managing the estate take time. The usual turnaround time for an assignment is about 9 to 18 months. It can take longer, particularly if the assignee engages in long drawn out litigation or collecting a stream of payments.

During this period of time, the assignee is holding onto the cash proceeds in an interest bearing account. Who gets the interest? Mind you, the interest is usually 1% to 1.5% at best, but money is money. If the cash deposits run in the millions, a few dollars here and a few dollars there adds up. Most assignment contracts award the interest on the deposits to the assignee as compensation for the assignee's services. Is this legal? Yes, because the debtor can set the terms for the assignee's compensation, which might include the accrual of interest. Is this standard? Yes. Does this matter? Maybe; if the amount of interest is large and the case has only a handful of creditors.

Here is the punch line. An ABC is cheaper to prosecute than a bankruptcy if the ABC consists of assets readily salable, if it is free of any apparent conflict among creditors, if the creditors are few in number, and if the estate is free of tax liability. Creditors would recover more than they would from a bankruptcy. On the other hand, if the case is complicated, full of fraudulent conveyances, laundered assets, encumbered property, and parties or creditors who are in conflict, the creditors will fare not better, or even worse, than in a full blown bankruptcy.

Priority of Payment

Here is the standard priority of payment in assignments:

A. Secured claims, which include interest, costs, and attorneys' fees to date.

B. Costs of administration, which include assignee's fees and charges, fees due the attorney for the assignee, accountant fees and costs of administration, and potentially fees claimed by the attorney for debtor.

C. Tax claims, which might include federal and state taxes, employment taxes (that bear horrendous penalties and interest), sales tax, and county and city taxes.

D. Statutory claims, including wages, union (trust, benefit, and health) claims, claims due the labor commissioner for wage claims, wage claimants, and other statutory claims.

E. Unsecured creditors.

Without a blow by blow description, this list tracks bankruptcy. In either case, creditors huddle at the bottom of the distribution well.

The Rights and Powers of the Assignee

What is the difference between Rambo and a bankruptcy trustee? Answer: You need subtitles to figure out what Rambo is saying. Sylvester Stallone mumbled his way through four *Rambo* movies. Otherwise, they are blood brothers.

The trustee can recover preferences, fraudulent conveyances, topple unperfected security interests, avoid post petition transfers, and exercise the "strong arm statute." The trustee stands in the shoes of the creditors and the debtor. The trustee can invoke the automatic stay. Judges appoint trustees from the standing panel, which is maintained by the U.S. Trustee. Trustees are bonded, policed by the U.S. Trustee, and make Caesar's wife look tawdry. Absent *Stern vs. Marshall* limitations, the trustee can file all cases in the bankruptcy court, which offers bankruptcy judges whose job is to adjudicate these cases. Assuming a successful outcome, the trustee enforces the bankruptcy court judgment which is, for all practical purposes, a judgment of the United States District court. If the debtor is a mess, bankruptcy is the best choice.

What about the assignee for the benefit of creditors? Some states (i.e., California Civil Code Section 1800) empower an assignee to recover preferences that mirror Bankruptcy Code Section 547(b). The cases are in conflict on this topic. Let's see what the assignee can do:

An assignee can recover fraudulent conveyances under the Uniform Voidable Transactions Act (California Civil Code Section 3439.01(c): "Creditor includes . . . assignee of a general assignment for benefit of creditors").

An assignment would terminate, automatically, an attachment lien and levy, if the debtor consummated the assignment within 90 days of the attachment (California Code of Civil Procedure Section 493.010 seq.). An assignee is a creditor under the UCC (California Commercial Code Section 1201(b)(13).

An assignee is a lien creditor under Article 9 of the UCC (California Commercial Code Section 9102(a)(52)(A)(ii)) and seeks priority against other lien claimants, or judgment creditors (or attachment creditors) who only filed a JL-1 (judgment lien) or AT-1 (attachment liens) with the secretary of state. A lien creditor takes priority over unsecured creditors and unperfected secured creditors. This is a big deal because the assignee assumes some of the rights and powers of a bankruptcy trustee under the "strong arm statute" (Bankruptcy Code Section 544: "creditor that obtains a judicial lien").

An assignee also stands in the shoes of the debtor, which entitles the assignee to sue the debtor's customers for unpaid bills; recover unlawful distributions and dividends, employee thefts, and defalcations; and pursue damage claims. Absent a special state statute that regulates assignments, the assignment contract itself and the state's trust laws embody the duties and conduct of the assignee.

In comparison, the trustee has additional rights and powers that the trustee may exercise in a specialized court before a judge expert in the area of law. As assignee might have many of the same rights and powers, but the assignee will slog its way through state court, which might have less familiarity with the body of law.

Nearly all trustees will invest the time and effort to review the debtor's records for any type of skullduggery. Trustees are duty bound to recover hidden and concealed assets. How about the assignee? Most assignments for the benefit of creditors transfer the debtor's assets to the assignee, who is contractually obligated to liquidate the assets and pay creditors. An assignee is also a trustee under general trust law, which is found in the state's trust or probate code. Rarely does an assignment contract itself actually compel the assignee to hunt through the debtor's records to gin up a fraudulent conveyance or theft of assets case.

Assignments are voluntary. No law compels the troubled debtor to proceed with an assignment. In nearly all cases, the principal of the troubled business retains expert insolvency counsel to advise of the options in liquidating the business. Chances are the principal might bear liability for an "insider preference," fraudulent conveyance, or downright theft of corporate assets. Filing a bankruptcy would deposit these big time claims into the hands of the trustee, who would be legally bound and ethically obligated to sue the liable parties. If the attorney suggested that an assignee might be slightly less diligent in pursuing the principal who might have robbed the company, expect the principal to choose the assignment.

Power of Subpoena

Bankruptcy Rule of Procedure 2004 offers subpoenas to the trustee, creditors, the U.S. Trustee, equity holders, or anybody else with a legitimate interest. A subpoena compels testimony and the production of documents held by the debtor or third parties, including banks, title companies, attorneys, business associates, or just about anybody else. Rule 2004 is the starter pistol in any quest to recover assets or gin up enough evidence to bar a discharge, exempt a debt from a discharge, or take any other civil action. Rule 2004 guarantees the "movie trailer" for the upcoming civil litigation.

Bankruptcy Code Section 341 compels the debtor to appear at the first meeting of creditors. The debtor must respond to the trustee and creditor's questions. Chapter 7 and Chapter 13 first meetings run about 10 to 15 minutes. Chapter 11 first meetings can go for hours or even days. These first meetings assist the trustee or creditor in evaluating a claim, locating assets, or initiating the quest to look for key documents. The first meeting is another opportunity to secure sworn testimony. The transcripts of the first meetings are available for a small charge or free.

Depending upon the state and the particular assignment, creditors and the assignee lack the power of subpoena. The debtor, its principals, and third parties are generally immune from any examination. Absent the filing of a lawsuit and ensuing discovery or agreement in the assignment contract, the debtor and the insiders are not obligated to answer anyone's questions or produce any records.

Why is this important? Without the testimony of the key players and documents at hand, the assignee faces a barrier in identifying assets illicitly taken by insiders. The assignee might not be able to identify what assets were taken, who actually took the assets, or snare evidence to justify suit. Without evidence in hand, the assignee would be disinclined to file any civil litigation seeking the recovery of looted assets.

Subordinating the Claim of an Insider

The explanation takes a little patience.

Here is our example, in order to set the stage. Our serial entrepreneur (Mr. Insider) forms TCC Inc. (a Thinly Capitalized Corporation), which manufactures widgets. Mr. Insider lends TCC Inc. $100,000 to pay utilities, leases, and workers' compensation deposits, and he takes a security interest for further advances and his wages. Mr. Insider opens up credit accounts with bobble head suppliers, including molds, plastics, paint, packaging, and labels. Mr. Insider has a hit on his hands. He sells out his entire stock. However, Mr. Insider declines to pay his suppliers, who are owed millions. The creditors sue. To stop the lawsuits, Mr. Insider puts TCC Inc. into a Chapter 7. The suppliers file their proofs of claims. Mr. Insider files his secured proof of claim for additional advances and his wages, whose amounts exceed the estate assets. If the claim of Mr. Insider is allowed, creditors get nothing.

These egregious facts enable the bankruptcy judge to subordinate Mr. Insider's secured claim to the claims of the unsecured creditors based on equitable subordination. *Taylor v. Standard Gas & Elec. Co.,* 306 U.S. 307, 323, 59 S. Ct. 543, 550, 83 L. Ed. 669 (1939) allows authorized subordination on these facts:

> Deep Rock finds itself bankrupt not only because of the enormous sums it owes Standard but because of the abuses in management due to the paramount interest of interlocking officers and directors in the preservation of Standard's position, as at once proprietor and creditor of Deep Rock. It is impossible to recast Deep Rock's history and experience so as even to approximate what would be its financial condition at this day had it been adequately capitalized and independently managed and had its fiscal affairs been conducted with an eye single to its own interests. In order to remain in undisturbed possession and to prevent the preferred stockholders having a vote and a voice in the management, Standard has caused Deep Rock to pay preferred dividends in large amounts. Whatever may be the fact as to the legality of such dividends judged by the balance sheets and earnings statements of Deep Rock, it is evident that they would not have been paid over a long course of years by a company on the precipice of bankruptcy and in dire need of cash working capital.

The court required that the plan subordinate the interests of Standard Gas & Elec. (page 324). In our hypothetical, a bankruptcy judge might subordinate the claims of Mr. Insider. The name "Deep Rock" is a buzzword for equitable subordination in bankruptcy proceedings. As a practical matter, equitable subordination accrues enormous legal expense because this litigation is fact driven, and the insiders will stoutly defend themselves. Armed with the power of examination and subpoena of records, the bankruptcy trustee can dig up the dirt that would justify "Deep Rock" subordination.

Mr. Insider has options. The attorneys suggest an assignment for the benefit of creditors. Why? First, the assignee lacks the power of subpoena (depending upon the state) and would face enormous obstacles in mounting a case. An assignment for the benefit of creditors is not a judicial proceeding. Next, assuming that the assignee has a decent case, the assignee would have to file a standalone state court action to seek equitable subordination. Most state court judges view these cases as "fish out of water." It is not even certain that the assignee would file the case in civil court; it could potentially file the case in probate court given that the probate court administers trusts. Certainly, Mr. Insider would demand that the assignee name all creditors in the lawsuit as necessary and indispensible parties, force the creditors to file answers at great costs, and even commence discovery. Mr. Insider will demand a jury trial. As can be seen, this litigation is becoming very expensive, which leads to a settlement or even abandonment lest the estate cash finance litigation with too little to show.

Filing the Claim and Claim Objections

In a Chapter 7 or 13, a creditor has 90 days to file the proof of claim. In a Chapter 11, the court sets the date, unless the date is announced in the first meeting of creditors notice, which is 90 days from the date of the first meeting of creditors. The courts establish the proof of claim form, which is provided to the creditors or available on line. The mega cases offer proofs of claim which are partially completed by filing in the name of the debtor and the case numbers. The courts appoint a claims agent to receive and docket proofs of claims, which enables a creditor to "fax file" the proof of claim. The claims agent also informs everyone of the bar date.

Trustees are duty bound to examine the proofs of claims. If some documentation is missing; or the proof of claim does not match the debtor's records, or the creditor received a preference; or the debt claimed by the creditor is barred by the statute of limitation, inflated, bogus or bad, then the trustee will object to the proof of claim.

What is a claim objection in bankruptcy court? First, the technical term is that a claim objection is a contested matter (i.e., a legal proceeding), and subject to the Bankruptcy Rules of Procedure and local rules. The trustee files a piece of paper with the bankruptcy court. This piece of paper says that the trustee declines to pay the proof of claim, states the basis of the objection, and provides a "drop dead date" for the creditor to file a opposition that responds to the claim objection. In most courts, this paperwork is a one page form. Most claim objections are resolved. Some creditors default because the amount of money is too small to justify hiring an attorney, or the creditor has written off the debt and does not care. No matter the outcome, the sole forum is the bankruptcy court, which expertly manages claim objections. In mega cases, the debtor might object to thousands (no typo here) of claims, which leads to waves of "omnibus objections" that might exceed hundreds.

On the other hand, assignments are a touch less precise. An assignee will set the date when a proof of claim is due. Some assignees offer their own form, which varies from assignee to assignee, but generally the proofs of claims parallel the bankruptcy version. The assignee warns the creditors that the assignee has imposed a "cut off" date, which means that a late filed claim will be kicked to the curb. (It is unclear whether the assignee can really impose a drop dead date under trust law, but this is another book.)

The stage is now set. Let's go back a trifle. We talked about the fact that the bankruptcy court is the forum in which a bankruptcy is conducted. Bankruptcy judges run a very tight ship. The trustee files claim objections, which are subject to very tight rules and clear drop dead dates. In response, the creditor files a memorandum and declaration, which attaches a document that refutes the claim objection. This is only a modest amount of paper. Filings are electronic. No one is paying a filing fee. The claim objection is set for a preliminary hearing in which the court sets the case for trial, unless the issue is cut and dry. The bankruptcy judge is highly motivated to expertly manage the claims objections, particularly in very large cases. In the mega cases, the debtor cycles through waves of objections.

An assignment is a private contract between the debtor and a third party that enables the debtor to transfer its assets to the third party (the assignee), who liquidates the assets and pays creditors. Depending upon the state, no papers are filed with the court. Depending upon the state, a judge does not supervise the assignment. The assignee does not file an accounting with the court. The assignee is not required to take any action unless mandated by the assignment contract or generally under trust law. In rejecting a creditor's claim, the assignee writes the creditor a letter that informs the creditor that the assignee declines payment and the reason. If the creditor wants to respond, the creditor has to (a) file an independent lawsuit in state court, (b) pay the requisite filing fee due the state court (about $300.00 to $500.00), (c) serve the lawsuit upon the assignee through the sheriff or process server, (d) calendar the initial status conference, (e) appear at the hearing, and (f) set the matter for trial in the state court. The assignee can reject a claim solely on the basis that the creditor's claim does not match the debtor's records. This is a big problem. Some debtors fail to keep any records. The records of some debtors are inadequate or incomplete. If the debtor keeps crappy books, the assignee compels the creditor to invest a boatload of money to prove up the claim. Many creditors walk given a $3,000 to $25,000 investment to prove up a claim in an insolvency proceeding.

Without too much legal scholarship, we can see that claim objection litigation from an assignment in civil court is a rare breed. Worse, the assignee might make a big stink that the venue for this claim litigation is the locale of the assignee (i.e., the big city) while the creditor might be located out of county, or worse, out of state. This is bad. If the claim is in the amount of $50,000 or less, and the dividend due the creditor is 10% on the dollar ($5,000.00), filing a state court action over a $5,000 dividend is not cost effective. To top it off, claim objections in an assignment are rare enough that the attorney would face a "learning curve," which is a buzzword for wasting the client's money in figuring out what to do.

More bad news plops on the creditor's desk. The estate funds finance claim objections. What does this mean? Say the assignee, through an attorney, no less, objects to a claim. ($400.00 to write the letter.) The creditor responds by showing proof that the claim is valid. ($400.00 to read the creditor's response.) The attorney replies that the debtor's records fail to substantiate the claim ($400.00). The creditor produces proof of delivery, the delivery manifest, the purchase order, invoices, and statement. ($800.00 to read everything.) The assignee stands on its position. (Another $400.00.) The creditor files suit in the local court, but the assignee moves for a change of venue ($2,500.00), which is granted. The court transfers the case to the assignee's locale ($1,000 for the paperwork). The assignee files an answer ($800.00) and proceeds with discovery ($1,600.00). After the deposition of the creditor, the assignee assures itself that the claim of the creditor is, in fact, valid. (Total bill: $6,900.00 more or less.) The assignee writes a check out of estate funds that diminishes the total due all creditors. Litigating over a $5,000 dividend in bankruptcy court might be cost effective, if settled quickly. Litigating over a $5,000 dividend in state court is not cost effective, without enormous efficiency.

Creditors likewise condemn claim litigation in bankruptcy court as wasteful and sometimes abusive. In some Chapter 11s, the debtor objects to every claim on the basis of "inadequate documentation," or "inconsistent with debtor's records." Many creditors decline to respond in the face of a small dollar dividend and big expenses. However, creditors, if truly bent out of shape, or if represented by a creditors' committee, can complain to the bankruptcy judge or the U.S. Trustee.

The Best Option (When All Options Are Bad)

Businesses fail for a million reasons, including bad management, inadequate capital, shifts in the marketplace, or just bad luck. An assignment might return a greater recovery to the creditors if the assignee can readily sell the assets, the liens are not disputed, and the case is free of internecine sniping between the debtor and its creditors. Freed of expensive oversight, the estate might generate a greater recovery than creditors would receive in a bankruptcy. On the other hand, a debtor repelling the barbarians at the gates, desirous of recouping money taken by levies and hoping to dump liens, belongs in bankruptcy court.

Do your part to make the best of an assignment: remember to timely file the proof of claim and periodically communicate with the assignee to get an update on the status of the case, including asset sales.

Do I Really Care About Pursuing This?

Assignments are not creditor friendly. Unlike bankruptcy, assignments do not offer creditors the power of an independent examination nor the power to produce records from the debtor or third parties. Assignees are disinclined to sue the principals of the assignor because assignees generate business when the insolvency counsel for the assignor recommends the assignee. Few attorneys would be willing to put the principals of their clients in the bulls eye of an expensive and possible ruinous lawsuit. Few assignees would pursue a *Deep Rock* claim. When a big time debtor assigns its assets to a neutral party for the benefit of the creditors, the debtor (and principals) are often hiding corporate malfeasance.

Does this make a difference to the individual creditor? If the total creditor body amounts to $5 million, and the estate consists, as reported, of $500,000 in assets, but the insiders looted about $100,000, then the theft, if recovered, only amounts to 2% additional distribution. Even if the insider theft was $1,000,000, the additional recovery would be only 20%. Insiders don't cough up embezzled funds without a big legal fight. Chances are good the assignee is going to spend 33.3% in legal fees to recover the $1,000,000, and the insider might settle at, say, $666,666.66. The net due creditors is $333,333.33, which is a 6.6% additional recovery.

The answer to the initial question is usually "not really" because although finding out what happened will be entertaining, the potential recovery due each creditor is diluted given the costs of recovering insider theft. Insolvency litigation demonstrates the law of diminishing returns.

Assignments succeed when the the case is bereft of fraudulent conveyances, concealment, and other misdeeds. If the debtor owns a valuable asset and wants to pay off creditors, an assignment is the best solution. If the case is a mess and buried under a pile of transfers, concealments, and bad record keeping (i.e., fraud and theft), bankruptcy is a better deal.

Now, all of that said, if the parties want a simple deal, the debtor can sell the business in a bulk sale. A bulk sale is a contractual transfer of the property, and we examine these in our next chapter.

11

Bulk Transfers

The Short Story

Synopsis

A bulk transfer is the sale of a business primarily selling goods or manufacturing that provides for notice to creditors, an escrow, and payment of claims. Very closely associated is California Business and Professions Code Section 24074, which requires parties to establish an escrow for payment of creditors' claims from the proceeds for all sales that involve the transfer of any liquor license (including beer and wine).

Legal Basis

Article 6 of the Uniform Commercial Code, if enacted. The common term is the Bulk Sales Act. Some variations also include escrow conducted under the auspices of the state's alcoholic Beverage Control Act that might establish an escrow for creditors. A cautious buyer might demand notice and escrow to insure that creditors "come out of the wood work" and receive payment of claims. Fearful of secret or undisclosed claims, hidden liens, or other horrors dropping from the sky, buyers can demand an escrow and notice to the creditors.

Is This a Good Law?

Many states have repealed their bulk sale laws (Article 6 of the UCC). However, California retains the Division 6 in its near original form.

When Do I File a Claim?

Within 12 business days—check with local statute. This is very short period of time, considering that notice is not electronic and that creditors might need time to gather key documents and time to physically file the claim.

What Does It Mean to File a Claim?

Use personal delivery, overnight services, USPS Express mail, and maybe fax. Email is uncertain, but you can try.

How Do I Locate the Filing?

It is difficult. Notice is published and recorded; notice is not sent to creditors, depending upon the state statute. Creditors should cull through the public records (i.e., the recorder) to locate the notice. Depending upon the state, some commercial services provide "alert" notices that might or might not be timely. If the creditor filed a UCC, the buyer or escrow holder will communicate with the secured creditor to obtain a lien release and pay-off.

What Do I File?

A letter specifying the amount, including the basis, total due, support documentation, and accruing interest (the rate and daily amount).

Do I Get Accruing Interest?

Yes, for secured claims. Yes, for unsecured claims if the estate is solvent. No, for unsecured claims if the estate is insolvent.

Do I Need to Update the Claim?

Yes.

Who Gets the Claim?

The escrow agent.

What Should I Include?

Everything.

Are There Privacy Issues?

Redact social security numbers, driver's license numbers, bank account numbers, and other clearly private information.

What Should I Expect from the Escrow Holder (and When)?

Acknowledgment of the claim within seven days. Ask for the acknowledgment. Confirm receipt.

Is There Judicial Supervision?

None, unless state enacted.

Is There a Risk of Side Deals?

Yes, a very high one. Unlike bankruptcy, which compel disclosures and enables the trustee to "reach back" to recover hidden or transferred assets, the bulk sale is a snapshot of the buyer's and seller's escrow instructions. The escrow does not reach a side deal, prior transfers, other viable assets, undisclosed assets, or even other proceeds due the seller, as specified in the agreement between the parties.

Are There Statutory Safeguards against Fraud?

None.

Can Another Party Object to My Claim?

Yes. The debtor can, another creditor can—and maybe for no reason at all.

If There Is an Objection, What Happens?

Depending upon the state, you might have to file suit and attach the dividend due you or your dividend will go to the debtor. The local statute might require that attachment within 25 days.

What Does the Escrow Holder Provide at Close?

A summary accounting of the sale proceeds (as disclosed by the parties in the escrow agreement only) going into escrow and proposed distribution to the creditor based on their classification. This is a *snapshot* the buyer and seller agreed to disclose to the creditors.

What Are the Priorities?

Taxes, wages, escrow and attorney fees, secured claims, PACA claims, statutory priorities, landlords' claims (maybe), U.S. government claims, claims of property owners, and—finally—unsecured creditors.

Do I Have an Obligation to Object to Another Claim?

You can object to a bad claim.

When Can I Object?

At any time.

Do I Have Remedies if a Bad Claim Has Been Filed?

File suit against the escrow holder, the debtor, and the claimant. You might be required to secure a restraining order. The escrow holder will typically either stand down pending resolution of the claim or file an interpleader.

What About Accuracy of Claims and Liability?

Absent general state law on fraud, Article 6 does not impose any specific liability for a bad claim. Depending on the state, the filing of the claim may or may not be a privileged communication, which raises issues of immunity.

Is Compliance with FDCPA Required?

Probably. This includes an entire body of federal and state consumer protection law.

When Do I See an Accounting or Money?

At close of escrow. State law might prohibit the escrow holder from any prior dissemination of information.

When Should I Expect Payment?

Absent some machinations, fraud, a battle among the creditors and the debtor, or a defaulting buyer, the average turnaround is about 30 to 60 days.

How Is Transparency?

Fair to poor, but it depends upon the escrow holder and local law.

What Are Some Other Options?

An involuntary bankruptcy or receivership.

Stay of Legal Proceedings?

No.

Guarantor Status?

Depending upon the guaranty, the failure to file a claim in the escrow might exonerate the guarantor based on the failure of the creditor to act diligently.

Overall Fairness?

Good, fair, and poor. Bulk sales enable the debtor to exert great pre-filing planning without any repercussions, control the escrow, approve insider or fraudulent claims, object to legitimate claims, and control the escrow holder.

Right to Declare an Exemption?

Not too likely because a bulk transfer is a voluntary sale.

Right of Reclamation?

UCC Code Section 2702 permits a creditor to claim goods sold within 10 days to an insolvent and further back if there is a misrepresentation in writing. If the debtor turns the goods into cash (very likely), the creditor is an unsecured creditor, even though the subject of a fraud. Division 6 does not offer a reclamation a special priority.

What Are My Proactive Strategies?

Given that title passes at close of escrow, the creditor can seek a prejudgment writ of attach that might encumber the assets that entitled the creditors to priority and secured status. Many credit applications, loan documents, or other papers offer the credit secured status, but a financing statement might, or might not, have been filed, or filed properly, including a fixture filing. Immediate filing of suit against the guarantor (the insider in charge of the escrow) might convince the debtor to allow the claim. In the face of a fraudulent, inflated, incorrect, or insider competing claim, be very prompt in objecting to the claim. Insider and fraudulent claims are common, given the lack of judicial supervision. Compare the claims with the debtor's financial statement. Rent claims are notoriously inflated. Depending upon the state, creditor categories might be limited to claims arising from the operation of the business at a specific premises, or claims subject to specific priorities and categories. Insider or large wage claims, claims by insiders of "loans" or "secured advances," or claims from related entities are the usual suspects. Ousting a competing claim frees up money for the creditors. Under Article 6, if enacted, the escrow might owe a duty to comply with the Bulk Sales Act to the creditors. Absent some statutory mandate, the escrow holder's duties run to the buyer and seller and not to the creditor.

The Long Story

What Is a Bulk Sale?

A bulk sale is the sale of a business in which the parties (buyer or seller) notify the creditors of the sale, the buyer deposits the proceeds with an escrow holder, and the creditors file claims. At the close of the escrow, the escrow holder passes title, and the proceeds are distributed to the creditors of the seller.

A bulk sale is statutory, or by agreement. Most, but not all, states enacted Article 6 of the Uniform Commercial Code, which embodies the Bulk Sales Act.

All states have their own alcoholic beverage protection acts, which are enforced by their own Departments of Alcoholic Beverage Control (ABC). Depending upon the state, a bar, restaurant, or other business with a liquor license requires an analogous escrow, opportunity for the creditors to file claims, and distribution of funds to creditors pro rata upon closing. Unlike the Bulk Sales Act, which is voluntary, and creditor protection mechanisms, compliance with the state's ABC escrow requirements are mandatory. The ABC escrow law compels the buyer to file and publish a notice of intention to buy, disclose the consideration in summary, and post the notice on the premise's door. Creditors, or for that matter, anyone else, can file an objection on any number of grounds.

Many states have repealed the original Article 6 of the UCC.

When to File a Claim?

A creditor must file a claim with the escrow holder on the date that is specified in the notice (Commercial Code Section 6105(b)). The duty to pay claims is found in Section 6106.2(b) as follows:

6106.2. (a) This section applies only to a bulk sale where the consideration is two million dollars ($2,000,000) or less and is substantially all cash or an obligation of the buyer to pay cash in the future to the seller or a combination thereof.

(b) Upon every bulk sale subject to this section except one made by sale at auction or a sale or series of sales conducted by a liquidator on the seller's behalf, **it is the duty of the buyer or, if the transaction is handled through an escrow, the escrow agent to apply the cash consideration in accordance with this section so far as necessary to pay those debts of the seller for which claims are due and payable on or before the *date of the bulk sale* and are received in writing on or prior to the date specified as the last date to file claims with the person designated in the notice to receive claims.** This duty of the buyer or escrow agent runs to each claimant timely filing the claim. [Emphasis added]

The due date for filing claim is the "date of the bulk sale," which is 12 business days from the date of the notice under Section 6105(b). The creditor is obligated to insure that the claim is received in hand on or before the date of the bulk sales. A claimant can fax, overnight, or personally deliver the claim. Using regular mail, or return receipt requested, bears risk given the slowness of the mail.

Most claims are in the form of a letter that spells out the amount due, interest to date, the rate of interest, accruing interest to the date of payment, and the address where payment should be sent. Invoices, statements, proof of delivery, purchase orders, and contracts should be attached if only to fend off an objection based on the lack of documentation. If the claim is secured, attach the filed or recorded UCC or mortgage, and the agreement that authorized security. The letter should demand priority of payment if the claim is secured and only offer a lien release if and when the claim is paid in full.

Request in the claim that the escrow holder acknowledge receipt of the claim and return the "receipted copy" by way of fax or email to insure that the claim was timely received. Overnight the claim via a commercial courier (Fed Ex, USPS Express Mail, UPS, DHL, etc.) to insure timely receipt and proof of delivery. Verify delivery actual delivery. A stitch in time saves nine given that the creditor only has 12 business days to get the claim to the escrow holder.

What Remedies Are Available to a Creditor to Gain Priority or Circumvent a Bulk Sale?

Let's walk back through this topic. A bankruptcy initiates legal proceedings that inject a trustee (or debtor in possession) endowed with statutory rights. The rights of the creditors are frozen upon the filing of the petition. Creditor cannot travel back in time to reconstitute their status from unsecured to secured. While a creditor might have reclamation rights and priority rights pre-petition, the filing of the bankruptcy slams the door in enhancing the status of the creditor. An assignment for the benefit of creditors, or equity receiver, likewise freezes the rights of the creditor, whether secured or unsecured, as of the date of the assignment.

Most bankruptcies, assignments, and receiverships do not drop from the sky. Creditors have some inkling that the debtor is going down the drain. Creditors have access to commercial credit reports, which reveal the barrage of collection lawsuits; IRS, state, and creditor liens; and even public announcements by the debtor. Creditors belong to credit associations that disseminate electronic information to their members. Some associations have monthly meetings in which credit professionals share information. In an attempt to fend off aggressive enforcement and buy peace, some debtors advise creditors of a pending bankruptcy or assignment and even the due date. This advance notice calms the waters because no creditor wants to spend money on a lawsuit that a bankruptcy or assignment would stop in tracks. Certainly, if the debtor is a public entity, or subject to the WARN ACT, the debtor would provide fair warning of a pending bankruptcy, assignment, or other proceeding.

Bulk sales are different. Granted that the actual date of the bulk sale when title passes is the point of no return—the commercial "crossing the Rubicon"—creditors get 12 days' notice under Section 6105(b)(1)-(2): 12 business days between the date of the recording and publication of the bulk sale notice.

What remedies are available to a creditor upon notice of potential bulk sale?

Option 1: File and record a UCC to convert the claim from unsecured to secured. How? Many sales agreements, credit applications, personal and real property leases, contracts, "terms and conditions," and invoices incorporate a security interest. Here is the short form standard language:

> Customer grants a security interest to seller to secure past, current and future obligations owed to the seller in all of the Customer's now owned and hereinafter acquired goods, wares, merchandise, furniture, fixtures, equipment, furnishing, leasehold improvements, leases, deposits, deposits accounts, bank accounts, accounts receivable, right to receive payment of money, cash on hand, proceeds from any sale, intellectual property, trade names, trademarks, copyrights, patents, commercial tort claims, general intangibles, property held as collateral with any lender, and all proceeds from the sale of any collateral thereof. The definition of Customer includes the Customer's divisions, subdivisions, subsidiaries, and acquisitions, no matter where located.

This is common language. Security agreements demanded in million dollar transactions can run 20 pages or more, but in the event of exigency arising from a potential insolvent bulk sale, any security interest is better than no security interest.

The creditor can unilaterally file or record a UCC if the debtor agrees to a security interest. Many commercial services will file and record a UCC on an expedited basis (within hours—not days). The total cost to file an UCC is less than $100. The filed UCC grants the status of a perfected secured creditor, which has priority over the unsecured creditors, unperfected secured creditors, junior lien creditors (including IRS later liens), and junior secured creditors. This is a very big deal. For $100.00 in filing charges, the creditor can move its claim from the bottom of the creditor totem pole to the top.

Before going on to the next section, let's stop the show here to review this term. A creditor is a "secured creditor" if the debtor grants a security interest, even though the creditor does not file a UCC. This is called, generally, an unperfected secured creditor, which takes priority over unsecured creditors. However, a perfected secured creditor (a filed UCC), or a lien creditor (trustee, assignee, equity receiver, creditor holding an attachment or execution levy) beats out a unperfected secured creditor. Filing a UCC does not require the debtor's permission. A creditor can file the UCC or have a commercial service file the UCC for the creditor, which is now the normal process. In a bulk sale setting, the creditor can file any time prior to the close of escrow, which would elevate the creditor's status to secured.

Insolvency is an ugly reality. Creditors bite the dust. Picture the gunfight at the O.K. Corral. A few souls didn't walk away. Good planning suggests that the creditor (a manufacturer, wholesaler, distributor, exporter, or financier of receivables) incorporate a security interest that might be perfected to insure priority in an ensuing bulk sale.

A security interest only requires words of grant, a signature, and a description of the collateral. (See UCC Code Section 9203(b)(1)-(3).) A Model T security interest is just as good as a Ferrari. There is a stripped down model that can be incorporated in even shorter language in a credit application, contract, invoice, sales agreement, or terms and conditions:

> Buyer grants seller a perfected security interest in now all owned and hereinafter acquired goods, bank accounts, equipment, leasehold interests and improvements, commercial tort claims, general intangibles, and proceeds from the sale thereof to secure any debt owed to the seller.

How about an anorexic security interest? Try something even shorter: "This note is secured by a Security Interest in subject personal property as per invoices" (*In re Amex-Protein Dev. Corp.,* 504 F.2d 1056, 1057 (9th Cir. 1974)). This was a winner. Remember, something is better than nothing, and nothing is awful.

How does this security work? For reasons of expense or inattentiveness, the creditor might overlook this hidden security interest. Presume this oversight. Upon notice of the bulk sale, the creditor can immediately file the UCC with the secretary of state and record the UCC with the county recorder. Remember, unlike under the old law, the debtor is not required to sign the UCC. The creditor can unilaterally sign the UCC. Most states accept electronic filings of a UKCC, which means that the UCC is filed on the date of submission, or even within an hour of the tender. Presto Gizmo! The caterpillar creditor becomes the butterfly secured creditor who is entitled to priority status in the bulk sale. This newly minted lien brings the bulk sale to crashing halt because the buyer demands title free and clear of liens. No buyer wants to buy a lawsuit. If the secured debt exceeds the sale price, the bulk sale dies on the vine until someone writes a bigger check. Alternatively, folks start talking about side deals.

The escrow holder is the agent for both the buyer and seller. Unlike a trustee in a bankruptcy, an assignee for the benefit of creditors, or an equity receiver, an escrow holder is not a "lien creditor" under UCC Code Section 9102(b)(52). The filing of UCC on the cusp of the bulk sale is valid. The filing even survives the close of the sale because the buyer takes subject to perfected liens.

Option 2: File suit and proceed to obtain an ex parte writ of attachment. This remedy presumes that the creditor cannot rely on a security interest. Many state statutes allow a creditor to seek a prejudgment writ of attachment if the defendant is selling its business. The statutory basis is typically (a) exigency because the debtor (i.e., the customer) is dissipating its assets in the bulk sale or the proceeds of the sale, (b), the local state statute might authorize a writ based on the sale itself or filing of a bulk sale notice, or (c) the inference of financial insolvency if the debtor is selling the business without paying the creditor's claims. The primary hurdle in obtaining an attachment, depending upon the estate, is the burden of paperwork, the amount of the bond, and the efficiency of the sheriff.

Writs of attachment are creatures of statute. Here is the drill: The creditor must file expeditiously and go into court within days to seek a court order that would authorize a lien on the assets or actual seizure of the assets. The creditor has to post a bond (which ranges from a $10,000 bond, in California, to a bond twice the amount of the claim or assets to be attached). If the attachment is granted, the creditor must get the sheriff (i.e., the levying officer) to take immediate action. Some sheriffs are more expeditious than others. Getting a court order for a writ of attachment might take more than a few days. If the escrow will close in 12 business days, the sheriff needs to act very quickly. The creditor should run a UCC search to insure that the assets are not already encumbered.

Writ of attachment proceeds are labor intensive and expensive. Writ proceedings become even more intensive and expensive in the face of heated opposition. Writ proceedings are unpredictable because some debtors just do not want to pay. Expect the debtors to bring some defense to the claim and argue that the writ would deprive the debtor of due process. ("I never got the product, and if I got the product, the product was defective . . . and if not defective, I already paid for it . . . and if you don't have my check . . . I will get enough money from the sale to pay you, but only if you dismiss the lawsuit . . .) The debtor might argue that sale would generate pennies on the dollar for each creditor and why give preference to the attaching creditor. Some debtors even rescind the current sale for the purpose of revamping the terms to redirect the proceeds to a third party or conduit for the benefit of insiders. Some debtors might file a protective Chapter 11 to stall off the writ proceedings. Don't expect the debtor to lay down and die. If the debtor is a natural person, the debtor can assert exemption rights.

What Is the Difference between a Bulk Sale, a Bankruptcy, and an Assignment if the End Result Is That Creditors Are Paid?

The Bankruptcy Code keeps creditors at bay, grants a discharge (if the debtor is a natural person), liquidates assets free of disputed liens, recoups preferences and fraudulent conveyances, and pays a dividend to the creditors. Bankruptcy is very expensive. Pennies on the dollar is the usual expectation. The trustee is a lien creditor, which gives the trustee the right to void unperfected liens that would free up money for the creditors.

An assignment liquidates assets, might recover some preferences or fraudulent conveyances, and pays creditors. If the estate is uncomplicated, creditors get more money than in a bankruptcy. Assignments are costly given the fees due the assignee and assignee's attorney. However, the assignee is a lien creditor, which enables the assignee to subordinate or void unperfected liens. Like a bankruptcy, the trustee (or assignee) sells the debtor's assets, but not free of liens, unless the assignee prosecutes its status as a lien creditor and avoids the liens.

A bulk sale is consensual sale of a business in which the seller and buyer agree to park the sale proceeds in an escrow, swap title at the close of the escrow, and pay creditors money on hand. If the business is sold without an escrow, and the buyer pays the seller, the buyer will be liable to the seller's creditors for what they would have gotten had parties complied with the Bulk Sale Act. Bulk sales are cheap.

What is generally similar to bankruptcy and assignment is the priority of payment, which is found in Commercial Code Section 6106.4(b)(2) as follows:

(1) All obligations owing to the United States, to the extent given priority by federal law.

(2) Secured claims, including statutory and judicial liens, to the extent of the consideration fairly attributable to the value of the properties securing the claims and in accordance with the priorities provided by law. A secured creditor shall participate in the distribution pursuant to this subdivision only if a release of lien is deposited by the secured creditor conditioned only upon receiving an amount equal to the distribution.

(3) Escrow and professional charges and brokers' fees attributable directly to the sale.

(4) Wage claims given priority by Section 1205 of the Code of Civil Procedure.

(5) All other tax claims.

(6) All other unsecured claims pro rata, including any deficiency claims of partially secured creditors.

This priority of payment is close to that of bankruptcy and assignment for benefit of creditors. Again, the bulk sale agent is not a lien creditor.

Bulk Sales Are a Creature of Statute

Article 6 of the UCC offers a statutory structure for bulk sales. The Bulk Sales Act establishes an escrow proceeding for the deposit of funds, and payment for greater, which immunizes the buyer from liability for creditor claims. Absent potential creditor's claims, or payment by the seller, parties can buy and sell a business without the necessity of compliance.

Typically, a buyer might insist on compliance with the bulk sales act to ward off claims by potential creditors even though the state law might not mandate a bulk sales. Nobody wants to buy a lawsuit.

However, the Bulk Sales Act is imperfect because, depending upon the precise state mechanism, the parties are not obligated to notify the creditors. The sole requirement is to publish and record a notice of bulk transfer notice. Granted that the recorded information becomes part of the public record, even in a digital world, notice is not a certainty. Publishing the notice in the local "legal" newspaper is unlikely to land a notice on the desk of the credit department of the major food wholesaler. Commercial services offer electronic notice of bulk sales.

While the parties might agree that the seller is obligated to disclose the identity of the creditor, the seller might default or have terrible books. In some cases, the seller is not aware of a creditor. In the entertainment business in major urban cities, some bars pirate boxing and sporting events, which leads to damage claims and money judgments. Some of these bars are run by absentee owners who might be unaware of these claims, which hover in the $25,000.00 range.

The ABC act is likewise a creature of statute. However, given the more controlled structure in the sale of alcoholic beverages and the small number of distributors, notice of a sale (and escrow) becomes common knowledge.

What Stops the Buyer and Seller from Engaging in a Side Deal?

Only a lack of ingenuity. Before explaining side deals, we are going to explain the "bumps and grinds" of nearly every business sale. The seller and the buyer of a business confront at least the following four issues.

Issue 1: Tax Consequences

The seller depreciated assets (equipment, leasehold improvement, goodwill, etc.) but if the seller sells these assets at a "big number," the seller might recapture the depreciation and pay capital gains tax. Let's say the seller purchases a tractor for $10,000.00 and during its life depreciated the tractor to $1,000.00. If the seller sold the tractor for $10,000.00, the seller made a gain, which obligates the seller to pay taxes, which might amount to some $3,333.33. Worse, the seller would have to pay sales tax based on the $10,000.00, which is about (depending upon the state) $700.00.

Likewise, the buyer asserts demands in the allocation of the sales price. The buyer would always prefer to allocate the sales price to assets, which are subject to depreciation, because the tax benefits effectively reduce the purchase price. Presuming that the seller completely wrote off the tractor as a 33% effective tax rate, the $10,000 price tag for the tractor means a $3,333.33 tax write off. Valuing assets drives present and future federal and state tax treatment.

Buyers and sellers look for all sorts of deals to alleviate the tax consequences. Let's keep in mind that the seller collects sales tax (depending upon the sale) for the sale "taxable assets," which is another expense borne by the seller. Framing the assets as intellectual property, a long term employment agreement, a covenant not to complete, or other "non tangible assets" might mitigate the sales tax consequences.

Issue 2: Cash Bookkeeping Concerns

The seller represents sales and profits greater than what the books show to the buyer. This is very common in a cash business. The books show $25,000 a month, which is barely breaking even, but the seller claims that the business generates $50,000 a month. Call the $25,000 of unreported income "soft income." The greater the income, the more valuable the business, by any standard. The seller is loath to admit (in writing) the skimming of the cash in light of the IRS's civil and criminal wrath. On the other hand, if paying a premium for a high income business, the buyer demands verification to prove this big income to verify the business will not turn out to be a bust.

The seller and buyer have to live with "two sets of books," which is clearly illegal.

Issue 3: Money Outside Escrow

The seller is a corporation or LLC. The principal of the seller did not sign any personal guaranties. The sole recourse of the vendors is escrow. The claims average less than $25,000 per creditor. The seller and buyer split up the sale proceeds. Half is paid prior the bulk sale (about 50% of the total) and the balance goes into escrow. Can the buyer and seller divert funds around a bulk sale? Maybe. Let's see what Commercial Code Section 6106.2(a). says:

> (a) This section applies only to a bulk sale where the consideration is two million dollars ($2,000,000) or less and is substantially all cash or an obligation of the buyer to pay cash in the future to the seller or a combination thereof.

> (b) Upon every bulk sale subject to this section except one made by sale at auction or a sale or series of sales conducted by a liquidator on the seller's behalf, **it is the duty of the buyer or, if the transaction is handled through an escrow, the escrow agent to apply the cash consideration in accordance with this section so far as necessary to pay those debts of the seller for which claims are due and payable on or before the date of the bulk sale and are received in writing on or prior to the date specified as the last date to file claims with the person designated in the notice to receive claims.** This duty of the buyer or escrow agent runs to each claimant timely filing the claim. [emphasis added]

Section 6106.2(b) compels the seller to pay its bills from the proceeds. Why? For what purpose? Face it, the seller has no love for its creditors. If the creditor's claims are not paid, the seller does not care because the seller's principal did not issue any personal guaranties. Moreover, the amount of the creditor's claims are too small to justify fraudulent conveyance or other litigation. Nobody is going to sue for fraud. This is a reality. Paying money outside or in advance of the escrow is a fact of life.

Issue 4: Long Term Employment Contracts

Bulk sales invite long term employment contracts. Unlike bankruptcy, bulk sales are private contracts, outside any judicial supervision. Parties can cook any deal they want. Creditors might carp, bark, and complain, but to unwind the deal, they have to sue the escrow holder, buyer, and seller. Suing costs money. Few creditors would spend big bucks when their claims are less than $100,000 because litigation offers no guaranties, other than the guaranty of paying the attorney. Embrace this reality because the client (a creditor) can file a collection lawsuit that enables the creditor to attach assets and compel payment as a priority claim in the escrow. Aware of these tricks to siphon funds around the escrow, the client (a vendor) can sell on COD terms, or impose a personal guaranty and, better yet, a perfected security interest.

Long term employment contracts cheat creditors. Here is how it works. The sale price is, say, $1,000,000.00. The seller deposits $500,000 into the escrow, which generates about a 33.3% return to creditors, which isn't a total disaster. The buyer pays the remaining $500,000 through a long term employment contract at the rate of $25,000.00 for a total of 20 months. The beneficiary of the employment contract is the principal of the seller.

Let's stop this show a second. Clearly the total $1mil should have gone in the escrow. Clearly, the $25,000.00 per month is part and parcel of the sale prices and therefore available to pay creditors. However, unless some creditor wants to invest real money in unwinding these shenanigans, this transaction will stand.

Why wouldn't creditor make a big stink? Channeling sales proceeds around the escrow holder through the guise of a long term employment contract is a fraudulent conveyance. The remedy, if granted, compels the principals (i.e., the insiders) of the seller to turn the long term employment into the escrow pot which would distribute the funds pro rata to the creditors. If the creditor is only owed, say, $100,000, or 10% of the total creditor pot, the creditor will receive pro rata payment from the added distribution, but subject to payment of its attorney's fees. If the creditor spends $50,000 on attorney's fees, but the added distribution is $50,000.00, the recovery is a wash. If the creditor spends $100,000 but only receives another $50,000, the recovery is a bust. Nice guys finish last.

A Bulk Sale Can Be a Fraudulent Conveyance

A bulk sale is a statutory means by which a buyer can compel the notice to creditors, establish an escrow, distribute funds to creditors, and escape potential liability for the seller's claims. A bulk sale immunizes the buyer from the seller's creditors. Sounds great.

What happens if the deal between the buyer and seller is a fraudulent conveyance? A fraudulent conveyance can be transfer of assets for less than fair and equivalent consideration when the debtor was insolvent or rendered insolvent. This is called a "constructive fraudulent conveyance" under the Uniform Fraudulent Transfer Act (UFTA; California Civil Code Section 3439.05) or the Uniform Fraudulent Conveyance Act (UFCA—which is the operative law in New York). The other, and more obvious, fraudulent conveyance is a conveyance made by a debtor with the intent to hinder, delay, and defraud present and future creditors. The concept of fraudulent conveyance dates back to before Queen Elizabeth I.

Just the fact that the parties to the transaction hired an escrow agent, published a bulk sale in a newspaper of general circulation, recorded the notice, and paid out whatever money was on hand does not immunize the transaction from a UFTA attack. If the deal is rotten, the deal is rotten, and it is subject to being toppled as a fraudulent conveyance.

In addition, the filing of bogus claims by family members of the seller, or entities created or controlled by the seller, are fraudulent conveyances. The "side deal" in which the buyer pays money outside the escrow might be fraudulent conveyance because the seller is channeling the side deal around the escrow and ostensibly beyond the reach of the creditors who filed claims.

Just Say No

Why are these homilies important in unraveling the mysteries of the dowdy bulk sale act? Here is the answer: the seller (who is the debtor) can reject every claim. Commercial Code Section 6106.2(c) provides as follows:

> If the seller disputes whether a claim is due and payable on the date of the bulk sale or the amount of any claim, the buyer or escrow agent shall withhold from distribution an amount equal to . . . 1) 125 percent of the first seven thousand five hundred dollars ($7,500) . . . and shall send a written notice to the claimant . . . unless attached within 25 days from the mailing of the notice. **Any portion of the amount withheld which is not attached by the claimant within that time shall be paid by the buyer or escrow agent to the seller, or to**

the other claimants in accordance with subdivision (b) of Section 6106.4 if they have not been paid in full . . . [emphasis added].

The seller will reject all claims without regard to whether the seller owes (or does not owe) the debt. The seller just says "no," rejecting the claim. Why? The answer is that the seller can. The Bulk Sales Act does not condition the rejection on any legal basis.

Will the creditors attach their pro rata proceeds? Is the attachment worth their while? First, collection lawsuits that require an attachment require at least a $2,000 to $3,000 cash investment for costs, plus fees, which consist of filings fees, service of process, the bond premium, levy fees, expensive overnight mail, and other miscellaneous "waste of money" expenditures of attorneys. Attorneys charge anywhere between 25% and 35% for their services on a contingency fee basis. If an attorney were hired on an hourly rate (say, $250.00 an hour), the fees would average about $2,500.00 to $3,000.00 just to get the attachment. If the creditor's pro rata distribution is less $10,000, it is unlikely to file suit, attach the pro rata, and litigate the case to judgment.

Do the math. The seller profits by rejecting any claim on the premise that few or no creditors are going to file suit and attach. Given the absence of creditors, the escrow holder remits the total sale proceeds to the seller.

Speak Up or Forever Hold Your Peace

Lots of creditors file claims. Vendors file claims for goods and services. Landlords file claims for past due and even future rents, if there is a lease default. Taxing authorities claim unpaid sales tax, withholding taxes, and property taxes. Investors assert claims for unpaid loans, profit participations, or even a security interest in the business. The principals of the seller assert large unpaid wages and, better yet, assert a statutory priority. More bizarre creditors drop from the sky. They include hard money lenders who assert an interest in everything to repay the last minute loans. Union trust funds, for pensions or health care or other benefits, file claims. ASCAP asserts claims (demanding music royalties). Boxing promoters assert claims (for cable television piracy because the seller, a restaurant owner, showed a licensed boxing event without payment).

Most of these claims are valid, but some claims are bogus, false, inflated, or mischaracterized. All insider claims are suspect. Landlord claims for future rent are suspect. Long term contract claims are suspect. Investor claims are always suspect. The escrow holder is not authorized to reject a claim. Only the seller can reject the claim. At the close of escrow, the escrow holder sends out a notice of pro rata distribution under Section 6106.4(a)(2)&(3) as follows:

> (2) Within five business days after the time the bulk sale would otherwise have been consummated, send a written notice to each claimant who has filed a claim stating the total consideration deposited or agreed to be deposited in the escrow, the name of each claimant who filed a claim against the escrow and the amount of each claim, the amount proposed to be paid to each claimant, the new date scheduled for the passing of legal title pursuant to paragraph . . .

> (3) If no written objection to the distribution described in the notice required by paragraph (2) is received by the escrow agent prior to the new date specified in the notice for the passing of legal title, **the escrow agent shall not be liable to any person to whom the notice required by paragraph (2) was sent for any good faith error that may have been committed in allocating and distributing the consideration as stated in the notice**. [emphasis added]

If no one objects to the proposed distribution, the escrow holder can distribute the funds even though some of the claims are false, fraudulent, or bogus. A creditor might sue the other creditors for a fraudulent conveyance, but this is a total non starter because the individual's recovery is limited to the increase in the dividend due the creditor had the bogus claim not been paid. This is very small money, or no money, given the litigation costs.

Trying to intuit which claims are false, inflated, fraudulent, or fabricated from escrow statements, at best, is very difficult. Many times, it is just guess work.

What Does a Creditor Get if the Seller and Buyer Skipped the Bulk Sales Act?

The short answer: Not much. The short answer is that the measure of damages is equal to what the creditor would have received had the parties complied. If the creditor is owed, say, $50,000.00, but the seller is completely insolvent, and the creditor would have gotten no more than $5,000.00 through a bona fide escrow under the Bulk Sales Act, the creditor's damages are $5,000.00. See Commercial Code Section 6107(a) as follows:

> Except as provided in subdivision (c), and subject to the limitation in subdivision (d), a buyer who fails to comply with the requirements

of Section 6104 with respect to a claimant is liable to the claimant for damages in the amount of the claim, **reduced by any amount that the claimant would not have realized if the buyer had complied**. [emphasis added]

The technical term is "chump change." The buyer is entitled to the "good faith" "attempt to comply" defense under Section 6107(c) as follows:

(c) **A buyer who made a good faith and commercially reasonable effort to comply with the requirements of Section 6104** or to exclude the sale from the application of this division under subdivision (c) of Section 6103 is not liable to creditors for failure to comply with the requirements of Section 6104. The buyer has the burden of establishing the good faith and commercial reasonableness of the effort. [emphasis added]

The good faith defense will let the buyer off the hook and make litigation expensive, fact specific, and very problematic.

The statute of limitations is one year to bring an action against the buyer (Commercial Code Section 6110). Non compliance will not topple the transaction, nor avoid the sale, rights in the hands of the buyer. See Commercial Code Section 6107(h)(1)-(4), as follows:

(h) A buyer's failure to comply with the requirements of Section 6104 does not do any of the following:

(1) Impair the buyer's rights in or title to the assets.

(2) Render the sale ineffective, void, or voidable.

(3) Entitle a creditor to more than a single satisfaction of its claim.

(4) Create liability other than as provided in this division.

Famous Movie Lines That Might Be True: "Trust No One"

Bulk sales facilitate the sale and transfer of businesses and payment of creditors' claims. The Bulk Sale Act, found in Division 6, works pretty well, except when the Bulk Sales Act does not work at all. Most, if not nearly all, bulk sales going through an escrow deliver what is statutorily promised to creditors, which is full payment or partial payment accompanied by a bona fide accounting. Bulk sales are cheap, efficient, and deliver title to the buyer and money to the creditors.

Bulk sales are generally honest. Escrow holders, who are licensed and bonded, work very hard to insure that the creditor gets what the Bulk Sales Act promises. Experienced escrow holders shy away from crooked deals.

However, given the lack of any court supervision and the normal machinations of "mice and men," some sellers pervert the process to cheat creditors, the tax authorities, their investors, and even the buyer. Here is where the Bulk Sales Act lacks an accessible enforcement mechanism to combat blatant fraud. While in most cases, fraud is the exception and not the rule, in a case where the seller is clearly insolvent and every dollar counts, the likelihood of fraud and abuse is high.

12

Probates and Trust Proceedings

The Short Story

Synopsis

Probate and trust proceedings administer the decedent's or trustor's property pursuant a detailed statutory process. The proceedings provide for payment for timely filed creditors' claims if assets are available. Probate provides for the sale of real and personal property, impounding the money and paying priority claims, administrative claims, "end of life" medical expenses, funeral and related expenses, taxes, and other like charges; the widow's exemption; and, finally, the creditor's timely filed claims. The purpose of the probate court, generally, is to provide a forum that would ensure that the testator's or trustor's instructions are fulfilled.

Legal Basis

Every state has enacted a detailed and very comprehensive probate code, which includes provisions for administration of trusts. Probate law is generally uniform as most probate codes follow the Uniform Probate Code. Trust law is also uniform and very old. The rights of heirs (the core of probate) is a very old concept and dates back to King Henry II (1133–1189). A judge in King Henry II's court might need a little refresher but could hold court today without too much effort. Deeds executed under court order are in every property's chain of title, somewhere in time. At one time or another all real property passes through the probate court.

Perhaps even more than traffic court, probate court touches everyone's life given that the estates of many folks are resolved in probate court. From the viewpoint of the law profession, estates and trusts are a unique legal specialty. Law libraries (paper and digital) warehouse endless shelves of treatises, practices guides, and other authorities.

When Do I File a Claim?

Each state offers specific deadlines to file a proof of claim with the court. Assuming timely notice, the creditor usually has 60 days to file the proof of claim. Absent notice, the time to file is 120 days after the letters of administration were issued. Check with local state law.

These are dates very certain. Some jurisdictions might allow for a late filed claim, but this will take a full court press and a very good excuse.

What Does It Mean to File a Claim?

Use personal delivery, overnight services, or USPS Express. Send the original and four copies or more. Enclose a fully self addressed envelope. Some courts are electronic, which enables the creditor to confirm timely filing.

Confirm the court address. This might sound simple, but sometimes the probate court is in a different building or has its own clerk. Big city courts sometimes occupy several buildings (i.e., civil court, criminal court, probate court, traffic court, family law court, etc.).

How Do I Locate the Filing?

This is easy to moderately challenging. Absent actual notice, the court dockets are online in most courts and can be searched by the person's name. The fact that the person is deceased is generally available online or through a search via Westlaw, Lexis Nexis, or other services.

What Do I File?

Probate claims are pre-printed forms available online. They are easy to complete. These claims are physically filed with the court. File the statutory request for special notice of papers filed by anyone. The failure to file a request for special notice is the number one error of attorneys responding to a probate or trust proceedings. Mail the notice to everyone and anyone who is a creditor, the attorneys, the estate administrator. Periodically check the docket (which is probably online) to make sure that you are getting notice of all papers, pleadings, and hearing dates. Notice of the proceedings is paramount. Absent notice, you will be blindsided through the machination of others, guaranteed.

Do I Get Accruing Interest?

Yes, for secured claims, which means that the claim is secured by an interest in real or personal property, including, for example, a mortgage, deed of trust, or security interest in personal property.

Yes, for unsecured claims if the estate is solvent. No, for unsecured claims if the estate is insolvent.

Do I Need to Update the Claim?

Yes. The failure to update a claim is an error that might deprive the claimant of the right amount. Make sure the accrued interest, accruing interest, penalties, points, reinstatement fees and charges, and attorney's fees are stated clearly.

Who Gets the Claim?

The court, the estate administrator (i.e., the executor, administrator, trustee, etc.), the attorneys for the administrator, and any party requesting special notice. This is a common error: failing to serve everyone.

What Should I Include?

Everything. Be very thorough and attach all documents to support the claim. Probates can drag on for years. Years later, when the probate is ready to pay creditors, those required supporting documents might be lost or destroyed.

Are There Privacy Issues?

Redact social security numbers, driver's license numbers, bank account numbers, and other clearly private information of all parties, dead or alive. Even when the person is dead the estate might hold a limited right of privacy.

What Should I Expect in Response (and When)?

Acknowledgment of the claim from the court within a few days. Be vigilant for the proof of filing. Confirm receipt.

Is There Judicial Supervision?

Judicial supervision of the proceedings is extensive. The estate administrator cannot sell, transfer, or dispose of assets without court approval. The short summary is that the judge approves the conduct of the administrator. Court hearings are routine. Accountings are detailed driven. The probate courts are vigilant in protecting all parties.

Is There a Risk of Side Deals?

Rest assured that the decedent, absent a sudden unexpected death, spent years in getting property to the beloved persons (or entities), cheating creditors and despised family members, and engineering a scheme to avoid state or federal or estate taxes (federal estate taxes are always in political play). Estate administrators lack the right of claw-back absent a fraudulent conveyance (and only if allowed by statute). Expect side deals made by family members to victimize other family members.

Legions of attorneys specialize in trust and estate planning (pre and post death) to avoid payment due creditors, the IRS, and specific family members. Estate planning attorneys wave goodbye to the dying as they enter financial nirvana. Expect the family members to break open the safe deposit box. While the dead care about family (some of them, at least), they readily jettison their creditors. Estate administrators likewise lack the bankruptcy strong arm and similar powers. However, an estate administrator can pursue a fraudulent conveyance.

The surviving family members are generally alert to the presence of the creditors and might be more than willing to conceal the decedent's assets.

Are There Statutory Safeguards against Fraud?

This question offers many answers. Sometimes, executors, administrators, trustees, or estate professionals are corrupt and embezzle from an estate. Surcharging these individuals is common in probate court. On other hand, the decedent might have compelled the executor or trustee to be bonded, or the court can order a bond. In many cases, the bond would pay the estate for any losses arising from the executor or trustee's fraud or theft. Embezzlement and theft from an estate does take place, particularly if a family member has a substantial drug or addiction problem.

Prior to death, the decedent, if seeking to protect his or her family from creditors, is inclined to fraudulently convey all property, including cash, accounts, and personal and real property. Unwinding these transfers can be difficult, expensive, and problematic.

Can Another Party Object to My Claim?

Maybe. If so, it will probably need court approval. Check with the local statute. This might happen if the estate is solvent and the children, or third parties, seek to siphon off money by filing an inflated claim.

If There Is an Objection, What Happens?

If the executor or other party objects to a creditor's claim, the creditor must file suit within the time allowed under local law, which is probably 60 to 90 days. File a copy of the lawsuit in the probate court, make sure it is timely, name the right party, and serve everyone very quickly. These are drop dead dates.

What Does the Estate Administrator Provide at Close?

If it is a probate: a statutorily mandated accounting. If it is a trust administration: potentially very little or nothing at all. The trustor can set the ground rules, which might limit the trustee in making disclosures. Hopefully, if there is money in the estate after payment or statutory probate fees and charges, professional fees and charges, priority claims, the widow's allowances, medical and funeral expenses, taxes, and secured claims, the creditor might get something.

What Are the Priorities?

Taxes, wages, attorneys' fees, secured claims, widow's exemption or statutory rights (if any), statutory priorities, funeral expenses, medical expenses, landlords' claims (maybe), U.S. government claims, statutory lien claims, and—finally—unsecured creditors.

Do I Have a Right to Object to Another Claim?

You can object to a bad claim filed by another but probably only with court approval. A bad claim one made for the purpose of draining money out of the estate.

When Can I Object?

Prior to the close of the case; any specific date is set by statute. Objecting to a disbursement is another "date driven" filing. Unlike other legal process, probate court is "form driven," and any practitioner should be alert to filing and serving the correct form on time.

Do I Have Remedies if a Bad Claim Has Been Filed?

Demand that the estate administrator object. Absent compliance with the demand, ask for court authority (if required) to file an objection to the claim. This is rare, but less rare in a solvent estate burdened with many creditors.

What About Accuracy of Claims and Liability?

Probate claims are filed under penalty of perjury. Absent the most brazen fraud or a prosecutor with time on her hands, fraud goes unpunished. However, the estate administrator is duty bound to police the claims. Accuracy is good. Inaccurate claims are bad.

Is Compliance with FDCPA Required?

This person is dead, but watch compliance with HIPAA. Also, be wary of the rights of privacy of spouses, children, and other persons associated with the decedent.

When Do I See an Accounting or Money?

Aside from *Bleak House*, probates and trust proceedings are notoriously slow. Expect 24 to 36 months to pass. You are entitled to an accounting. Courts demand and will compel an account from the estate administrator— down to the last penny. A court can surcharge an estate administrator for the unlawful taking of money or other professional misconduct, including the failure to keep records of property, the failure to timely file suits or other actions, the failure to invest funds in an appropriate account, the failure to insure or safeguard an account, the failure to file tax returns, or the mismanagement of assets. (And this is the short list.)

When Should I Expect Payment?

To give you an idea: 12 months is warp speed in probate court. Anecdotal and completely unscientific guess: between 12 and 48 months. If the probate is uncontested and consists mainly of cash, it might make an early distribution.

How Is Transparency?

During the proceedings, probate mandates very good transparency. However, if a trust proceeding or a trust is involved, or there was prior extensive estate or trust planning, expect zero transparency. Trusts hide property from others, including creditors. Armies of attorneys, over many centuries, developed strategies to use trust to beat out ex-wives, children from various marriages, creditors, partners, the IRS, and law enforcement.

Before the probate, transparency is zilch. The family, dying patriarch, care givers, professionals, and groupies know the "end is near." As the end approaches, some parties "accelerate" bequests by walking out with property to deplete the estate or steal from other heirs. Co-holders of safe deposit boxes empty out the contents. Bank accounts are down to zero. Decent art takes wings. Cars are re-registered. Wallets and purses disappear. Kiss the family jewelry goodbye.

What Are Some Other Options?

There isn't much, but bring a checkbook full of money. All proceedings that seek to unwind fraud, abuse, or theft in a probate or trust setting are time consuming, expensive, and require counsel with a high degree of expertise.

Stay of Legal Proceedings?

No. A co-obligor is subject to a lawsuit.

Guarantor Status?

Depending upon the guaranty, the failure to file a claim in the escrow might exonerate the guarantor based on the failure of the creditor to act diligently.

Overall Fairness?

Good, absent a scheme to cheat everyone, during the judicial proceeding for a trust or decedent estate. Bad to worse for any pre-proceeding planning. The major risk is when the decedent selected a family member to act as an estate administrator who is troubled or has substance abuse issues.

Right to Declare an Exemption?

The probate code accords the surviving spouse a broad "widow's" exemption, which depletes the estate.

Right of Reclamation?

UCC Code Section 2702 permits a creditor to claim goods sold within 10 days to an insolvent and further back if there is a misrepresentation in writing. If the debtor turns the goods into cash (very likely), the creditor is unsecured creditor, even though the subject of a fraud perpetrated by the debtor.

Archeological efforts akin to discovering King Tut's tomb might be required to unearth a UCC 2702 case in a probate court. Those with time on their hands can undertake this search. Reclamation in probate proceedings is possible, but very unlikely. Few elderly folks run an active business, but nonetheless, the a reclamation case is not impossible.

What Are My Proactive Strategies?

Absent *Armageddon, The Walking Dead,* or *Ghost* scenarios, family members (the estranged ones) and creditors anticipate their debtor is close to exiting this world, so the early bird gets the worm. Securing a claim through a pre-judgment writ of attachment, or other legal remedies, is paramount. However, getting the cooperation of the decedent, who is typically an elderly person, might constitute elder abuse or elicit claims of undue influence, lack of capacity, or other claims.

Probate and trust proceedings are judicial in nature, but traditionally less than creditor friendly. Probate offers family members very broad exemptions that can diminish or even defeat creditors' claims. Without a request for special notice, the creditor might not be aware of the proceedings in the probate court that authorize these exemptions.

The Long Story

What Is Probate?

Probate (or the probate code) is a statutory creation that authorizes the appointment of a designated estate representative, usually chosen by the decedent, to carry out the direction of the decedent in his (or her) will. If the decedent died with sufficient property, but no will, the heirs can petition the court to commence a probate in which the court will appoint a personal representative to dispose of the property as allowed by statute.

The core body of law is the Uniform Probate Code and the probate code of the state. Many courts have very detailed rules of court that are controlling and very precise. Local courts have their own "local rules." Each state offers mandatory forms for the establishment of the estate, notices, request for notice, creditor's claims, objection to claims, sale of assets, etc. These mandatory forms are easy to complete. Depending on the court, some forms are "paper filed" and others are "electronically filed."

Probate is statute, rule, and local rule driven. Wills and trusts date back to King Henry II, like many other bodies of law. The case law is well understood. Warring heirs in the 12th century, if reanimated today, would find themselves at home in a 21st century probate court. This is not an embellishment. Heirs are active litigants in bankruptcy court, particularly if the decedent cycled through many marriages. In most cases, individuals with substantial property draw up a will to carry out their wishes for who gets what property upon the individual's death. Most folks give their property to family members, starting with spouses and children. Many individuals bequeath property to their alma mater, religious institutions, charities, and public service organizations. Most universities, museums, religious organizations, and non profits have entire departments that manage charitable bequests. Where probate and trusts sometimes go wrong is when the decedent got divorced and remarried, had another set of children, and failed to update the will or trust agreement. Other problem cases involve a document that was poorly written, or, worse, those in which the decedent lacked a will or trust.

Probate is a highly specialized body of law. Most attorneys who practice in the area of probate and trusts are professional, straightforward, and diligent in getting notice out to creditors for many reasons, the first of which is to insure notice is given and no one complains that they were excluded from the proceedings. Judges control professional fees due attorneys; hence, attorneys are diligent in complying with their statutory and fiduciary obligations. Probate has spawned many professional associations, multi-volume treatises, and copious law review articles.

Some probates are insolvent, which means that the creditors' claims exceed the total value of distributable property. Unlike bankruptcies, assignment, and bulk sales, probates are involuntary proceedings, but only in a limited sense. Nobody chooses to die, but most elderly folks make plans to shield their assets from claims of creditors in a probate, which includes surreptitious pre-death transfers or arrangements to make assets available to heirs outside of probate. These arrangements include trusts, among other devices.

The Creditors

If the heirs anticipate creditor claims, the heirs, even while the testator (a fancy word for an old person about to die) lives, will raid the estate. They will empty out the safe deposit box. They will empty out the bank accounts. Expensive furniture, furnishings, paintings, and cars disappear. Everything of value grows feet and walks out the back door. This is not a guess. The testator often acquiesces or even participates in emptying out the estate.

Many sophisticated parties, with some money at hand, establish a trust that siphons the assets around or "before" the probate estate. While it is possible to reach assets in a trust, the creditors are obligated to sue or take other extraordinary action to reach these assets. Few creditors will commit to spending $20,000 or (a lot) more to reach assets buried in a trust when they might not be successful at all. The issue here is not necessarily the legal right to recover assets that have been hidden, transferred, or concealed in a trust, but whether the creditors are going to invest real money in recapturing assets.

The question of investment in litigation to capture assets goes to the heart of all asset protection schemes. Asset protection means a transfer of title, but not beneficial interest, to a nominee who is controlled by the debtor or the debtor's surrogate. The simplest asset protection is just changing the name of the business, changing the name on the bank account, or closing the account and transferring the funds to another bank across town, across the state, or across the country. Transferring property to spouses, children, a trust, LLCs, corporations, or offshore entities are all fraudulent conveyances. Cashing out bank accounts or checks are fraudulent conveyances. No doubt that all these transfers can be set aside. The body of law is the Uniform Voidable Transactions Act, formerly known as the Fraudulent Transfer Act or the Uniform Fraudulent Conveyance Act (still good in NYC).

All this being said, the purpose of the probate is provide for an orderly means to pay creditors from the available assets of the estate.

Caregivers, Insiders, Unhappy Children, and Thieves

Elderly folks are vulnerable to caregivers and unhappy adult children. Jewelry, mink coats, expensive clothing, fancy shoes, high end leather goods, electronics, and everything else that is portable might walk out the back door before the personal representative shows up at the front door. Kiss the decent art goodbye. Post death looting is an expectation, even at the hands of family members. When the last parent dies, siblings with a long memory and brewing hatred will take everything and anything of value. Not everyone is bad person in a family, but when an elderly person is near the end, a smart personal representative starts the process, pre-death, of removing valuables. This is a terrible reality that must be communicated to the creditors and third parties.

Adult children with drug problems or gambling issues are the locusts of any family probate estate. Everything goes out the back door. The black sheep of the family is also the bad sheep of the family.

Notice to Creditors

Unlike other bodies of law, probate is state specific, although most states draw on the Uniform Probate Code. The general rule is that the creditors are entitled to actual notice of the proceedings, which includes notice that a probate proceeding has been initiated and an opportunity to file a creditor's claim. If known, the estate professional (usually the executor, e.g., the personal representative) is obligated to mail notices to the known creditors. Most personal representatives will do so.

Nearly every state requires publication of the probate, which provides notice to the creditors who are unknown. The notices are published in a newspaper of general circulation, which is typically the local "legal newspaper." Today, these ads are online. The creditor might be able to locate the notice through an online search, and obituaries are also online.

Most probate dockets today are online, offering access to the creditor, who would be able to file a creditor's claim. Most search services, including Westlaw, Lexis Nexus, etc., identify the probate. Calling up the family members might be in order.

The Role of Personal Representative

Similar to a bankruptcy trustee or an assignee, the personal representative is obligated to liquidate the assets of the estate, pay claims of administration and taxes, pay the professionals (with court approval), and distribute the proceeds to creditors who have timely filed claims and whose claims have been approved. The personal representative is an estate fiduciary and potentially bonded, unless the bond was waived in the will.

The personal representative has the power and duty to review all claims. The personal representative can reject claims if they are wrong, overstated, barred by the statute of limitations, or on other legal basis.

Most wills waive the bond of the personal representative. This is a mistake front and center. Put a whole bunch of money in front of someone who is inexperienced, and nobody knows what will happen. If the decedent died intestate (a fancy word for "no will"), the court will appoint a personal representative and impose a bond. The county offers a public administrator. Many counties have network of professional (and bonded) fiduciaries who serve as personal representatives in probates, trustees of trusts, and conservators.

The Creditor's Claim

Most states offer their own pre printed form of proof of claim, which resembles a bankruptcy proof of claim. These are all pre-printed forms. These are the paramount issues:

A. Clearly identifying the basis of the claim, e.g., sale of good, rendition of service, loan of money, construction work, etc.

B. Attaching the key documents (copies, not the originals) that support the claim, including copies of documents that support a security interest.

C. Correctly and accurately calculating the balance due. Consider a creditor's claim a complaint in a lawsuit that spells out the claim, and relief sought, by the claimant.

D. Correctly identifying the creditor, which includes the legal name of the creditor, the name of the representative (attorney or agent), address, telephone number, email, and other contact information. This might sound obvious, but this is not obvious because the correct creditor has to timely file.

E. Service upon the personal representative and attorney, and filing of the creditor's claim with the court. Many attorneys fail to serve the personal representative.

F. The filing of the creditor's claim is very time sensitive. Depending upon the state, the creditor's claim is due 60 days from the notice from the probate court or 120 days from the date of the the issuance of the letters testamentary. These are dates that are certain. Avoid mailing the creditor's claim to court; rather, use overnight services to insure that the court receives the creditor's claim. Include in the envelope the original and four copies, plus a self addressed return envelope. Most courts are online, which enables the creditor to confirm that the claim has been filed.

G. If the attorney for the creditor moves, retires, or the law firm changes its name, a claim objection, if served by mail, might bounce. This is a big deal because the estate administration is only required to serve a claim objection by mail, as opposed to service of process by hand. If the claim objection bounces, or gets delayed by forwarding, the creditor might suffer a default. Keeping the address on the claim current is paramount. This risk seems low; nonetheless, some probates take many years to resolve. A five year time period is not unusual. During the five years, attorneys and others move. A change of address might not have been filed with the court, and the change of address with the post office is only good for about six months. A creditor has 120 days to file suit or be barred.

H. While the decedent might have been one obligor, the death of one obligor does not toll the statute of limitations as to other obligor. Lawsuits must be filed on a timely basis. If the decedent is currently a part to litigation, the plaintiff must file a motion to substitute in the personal representative as party and continue with the litigation either as the plaintiff or the defendant. Dead people cannot sue and dead people cannot defend. If an estate has not been established, the attorney for the parties might need to to install a personal representative to stand in the shoes of the decedent either as the plaintiff or as the defendant. If the decedent is a defendant in a lawsuit, the plaintiff should file a probate proof of claim in the case. This is a common and tragic error. Just substituting in the personal representative is not the same as filing the creditor's claim. When in doubt, file the creditor's claim timely and accurately. Suing the personal representative might not be the same as filing a proof of claim.

I. Some courts charge a filing fee in order to file a probate creditor's claim. The court might require a cashier's check or money order. This is trouble. Absent good diligence to double check the local rules of court, many attorneys present the creditor's claim for filing but find it is bounced back for the lack of a filing fee. If the creditor's claim is tendered on the last day to file, the return, unfiled, of the creditor's claim is a total disaster. The antidote is always to check with the local rules to confirm whether a filing fee is required and the method of payment and always provide a return envelope.

J. Interest might accrue on the claim if the estate is solvent. If the estate is insolvent, the general rules of equity stop the accrual interest on the date of death or on the date of probate. If the claim is fully secured, the creditor is entitled to interest to the date of payment, along with attorney's fees and costs.

K. Specify whether the claim is secured, state the nature and extent of the security, and attach the supporting documents.

Request for Special Notice

Aside from timely filing a creditor's claim, file a request for notice of all matters. This is a pre-printed form that simply requires you "check the boxes."

The request for notice compels all files to "paper serve" all pleadings, motions, sale notices, application for compensations, distribution of funds on hand, abandonment of assets, allowance or professional fees and expenses, applications for court order approving a settlement, and just about anything else. This might even include a settlement that distributes a large portion of the estate to third parties or a collusive claim settlement. A request for special notice provides the eyes and ears of the creditors. Filing a request for special notice should not invoke a filing fee or other charges.

Failing to file and serve a request for special notice, aside from filing to file the creditor's claim on time, is the number one error in all probate management. Like bankruptcy, these notices are important because, most assuredly, somewhere in the fine print is some type of filing that will prejudice the creditors. The number two error is not reading all notices from the probate court. If the personal representative is a family member, and the heirs are family members, everyone is working diligently to squeeze out the creditors. Probate court, like bankruptcy court, can be unforgiving to creditors and third parties who did not file a request for special notice or who, worse, did not carefully read the paperwork generated in the case.

If the estate is insolvent, and the personal representative is aligned with the heirs, expect the parties to engineer a deal that would transfer valuable property out of the estate. If a dissident creditor lacks notice of this proceeding because the dissident creditor did not file a request for special notice, the insiders might prevail in legally diminishing the estate and destroying the value of the creditor's claims. The fact that a creditor has demanded notice itself is enough to put everyone on notice that the creditor will not tolerate estate misconduct.

Liens and Priorities

General unsecured claims generally bear the same priority unless a claim is secured by real or personal property. A pre-death judgment, if secured by an abstract of judgment, or a personal property lien with the secretary of state, can assert secured status. The proof of claim should be filed as secured; attach all supporting documentation. If the judgment is bereft of liens, the judgment stands in the same category as other unsecured debts. The moral of this tale is always record abstracts and liens. Upon sale of estate property, the personal representative must pay the secured debt, which includes judgment liens.

A secured creditor need not file a creditor's claim because the lien survives the probate proceedings. The deed of trust, mortgage, UCC (financing state), pledge, or other lien enables the creditor to compel payment upon the sale or transfer by the personal representative. Upon liquidating the security, the creditor could file a claim and attach all supporting paperwork, including the UCC filings.

On the other hand, most secured creditors file a creditor's claim, file a request for special notice, and, more important, participate in every hearing. Secured claims accrue interest and the rate might escalate given the fact that the debtor (now the decedent) defaulted on the loan. (Always remember that claims that arise from a financial transaction accrue interest. If the claim arises from a "hard money loan," and the borrower is deceased, interest will continue to accrue at a default rate, which might chew up the equity in no time at all. Expect rates of interest exceeding 15% or more, and interest that might compound or include penalty charges. While the borrower is dead, the borrower's high interest loan is continuing to accrue nearly usurious rates of interest.) The fact of metastasizing interest gives impetus to the personal representative to sell the property, which is the collateral, to reduce the pay out due the secured creditor.

While slightly off the beaten path of insolvency, in a time of rapid real estate appreciation, real estate speculators pack the probate sales. These sales are standing room only. Properties are frequently sold at these sales well above the listing price.

Rejection of Claims

Generally, the personal representative is the party who would object to a creditor's claim. In other cases, anybody can object as along they can show some standing. This is unusual because a party objecting to the claim necessarily would have to hire an attorney and bear the normal costs of litigation. Generally, all litigation in probate court is slow, expensive, and detailed. Threats of litigation are cheap to make. Probate litigators are expensive.

Objecting to the creditor's claims is easy. The objection is a pre-printed form. While the personal representative is duty bound to have a reason to object to the claim, this is not relevant because the creditor bears the affirmative burden to file timely suit against the personal representative and file notice of the suit in the probate court. The time to hire an attorney, research the case, and file suit is typically *90 days*. This is not a lot of time if the estate might be insolvent, the creditor's claim is troubled, and the creditor lacks the immediate financial ability to hire an attorney. Some personal representatives might reject every claim just to see who will file suit. If nobody files suit, given the expense, time, and effort, the personal representative has cleared out the estate of creditor's claims.

Is objecting to all creditors without any basis morally and ethically reprehensible? For sure, but this does not matter because the onus is on the creditor to timely file suit. Few judges could or would look behind this whole "credit cleansing" when in fact no creditor filed suit to preserve their status in the estate.

In some states, the suit against the executor is heard in probate court. In other instances, the case is heard in civil court. Most modern courts are unified, which means the "probate department" is just another courtroom in the court house. The plaintiff is required to timely file the notice of suit in the probate court in order to apprise the personal representative and others who have requested special notice of the pendency of the lawsuit.

Once a claim is rejected, the claimant bears the affirmative burden of proof by a preponderance of the evidence to prove up the claim in court. This is important. Just filing the claim is akin to planting the flag. The creditor's claim is a judicial statement: "I am here." If the personal representative declines to object to the claim (usually because the claim is valid), the claim is deemed allowed. If the personal representative objects to the claim, the creditor, like any other litigant, must prove up the claim. The moral of this story? File claims that the claimant can prove, which means that the creditor should have documentary evidence at hand and witnesses reasonably available.

Filing a bad proof of claim is bad because some states require that a signatory declares under penalty of perjury that the claim is valid. Accuracy and veracity are the watchwords.

Exemptions in Probate Court

The widow might be entitled to exempt both real and personal property, which would immunize this property from the claims of creditors, heirs, and third parties. While exemptions are statutory and an expectation of a creditor, nonetheless, these exemptions deplete the estate available for creditors. These are called widow's exemptions. While judges are required to act impartially and apply the law evenly and fairly, anecdotal evidence might suggest that the widows have the upper hand.

Exemptions are unique to each state, but the big picture is that the exemptions take priority over the allowed creditor's claims.

Trusts

Trusts enable a individual to dispose of property outside of probate. The trustor can transfer property to an adult child as the trustee, who is also a beneficiary under spendthrift provision. Upon the adult child's death, the property goes to his or her children. If the adult child has no children, the property goes to the settlor's grandchildren, charities, or third parties. Suffice to say, the subject of trust law fills up many shelves in law school libraries.

The purpose of most trusts is generally to remove property from the reach of creditors and permit the settlor to enjoy the maximum control over and access to the property for many generations to come. More than one tort claimant, trade or consumer creditor, taxing authority, or other creditor has confronted the ugly reality that a well heeled individual is judgment proof because his wealth is safely ensconced in a valid spendthrift trust. This "trust fund" baby might well wear the face of insolvency because this person might be buried under a mound of debt while living a luxurious life. From time immemorial, creditors have sought to topple trusts—with limited success, and only after spending a lot of money. A trust that protects property from the reach of creditors renders the beneficiaries insolvent because the beneficiaries have big liabilities but own virtually no property in their own names.

The typical creditors of trust beneficiaries are (1) tort claimants because the beneficiary lacked adequate, or any, insurance; (2) family lenders because no bank would lend to the beneficiary under a spendthrift trust; (3) trade, construction, and other liabilities when the creditor failed to double check their customer's true financial condition; and (4) family law creditors from the prior marriage. Family law creditors include unpaid spousal and child support and community property equalization payments.

Not all is lost. Most states compel a trustee or a beneficiary under a trust to issue a certificate of trust, which compels the trustee to disclose whether the trust is revocable or irrevocable and the terms of the trust.

We now leave the dead and re-enter the land of the living—no, actually, the realm of the Walking Dead. The next chapter explains the workouts, extensions, and pot plans that enable a distressed or failing debtor to make peace with creditors (while sometimes walking away with a few dollars in his or her back pocket). These workout arrangements are common, but the machinations are uncommon. Read on.

13

Adjustments and Workouts

The Short Story

Synopsis

As an alternative to bankruptcy or other formal proceedings, some commercial debtors offer to settle the claims of their creditors. The offers consist of (1) a payment program of a fixed amount over months, quarters, or years, with pro rata payment to each creditor providing for partial or full payment of debt; (2) a composition or pot plan that offers a percentage of the pot or percentage on the dollar to creditors in lieu of bankruptcy; (3) payments from percentage of gross or net profits over time from the debtor or debtor's successor; (4) payment of a one-time discounted amount. The debtor, the debtor's attorney (or sometimes a third party, such as a credit manager's association) makes these offers and manages these programs.

The machinery here is worth explaining. The debtor owes money to the creditor. This is a contractual obligation, which consists of an immediately enforceable obligation with a fixed amount. The debtor might have agreed, for example, to pay interest at 18% (a usual contract rate), to pay attorney's fees in the event of suit, and to issue a personal guaranty. These are all standard terms of commercial credit, bank loans, matured lines of credit, or just about any other commercial obligation. If the debtor and the creditor enter into a "workout agreement," in which the debtor agrees to pay these obligations according to some type of formula, the agreement might not specify whether the creditor has "swapped out the original obligation" or initiated a "new obligation" under the workout. This is called substitution and novation.

This workout might be a total disaster for the creditor should the debtor default. If there is a default, the creditor perceives that the creditor can immediately file suit on the original obligation. In response, the debtor might claim that the original obligation was "swapped out" and in its place is the "new obligation" under the workout. A creditor must carefully read the workout and specifically reject the "swap out." Any workout, from the viewpoint of the creditor, should preserve the creditor's right to sue. Moreover, in the event of a workout, the creditor is probably obligated to get the guarantor to consent, less the guaranty claim exoneration under the guaranty and discharge from any liability the guarantor might owe to the creditor.

Workout agreements are legal landmines with lots of unpleasant surprises. A workout requires enormous diligence to insure that the creditor, in the event of a default, escapes unharmed and uninjured. As they say in all spy movies, trust no one, including the person handing you the check to sign your name to some dense contract in tiny print—single spaced, two sided, and full of legalese.

Here the typical treats and tricks: The payments under the plan are a substitute for the original creditor's claim. The debtor conditions payments on the creditors waiving their personal guaranty and signing a general release that would waive any rights against corporate insiders for other claims, such as fraud, "alter ego," insider dealings, theft of company assets, or any other basis of personal liability. Some arrangements compel the creditors to waive security interest. This is a "read the fine print" moment.

Legal Basis

A debtor is free to make a deal. This is basic law of contracting. A creditor can accept a discount or agree to accept payment over time. The creditor, absent its own obligations (i.e., its other creditors), can waive a claim, waive security, or waive a personal guaranty. Here the law of common sense digs in its heels. Business people succeed when they sell to customers who pay their bills on time. Business people succeed because they follow their accounts receivable. If there is a default, the business person as a vendor will dunn the customer and, absent payment, will file suit or hire a collection agency. If the customer collapses, for whatever reason, instead of filing bankruptcy, the customer might offer a "workout."

The offer of a workout does not preclude the creditor from immediately filing suit and seeking an pre-judgment writ of attachment. Provisional remedies, like an attachment, enable a creditor to lien the debtor's assets and gain priority. Depending upon the state, an attachment enables the creditor to seize inventory; encumber equipment, real property, or rolling stock; seize bank accounts, money market accounts, and stocks; and levy the accounts receivable. The writ of attachment is the core remedy here.

From the viewpoint of the debtor, "a debtor may pay one creditor in preference to another, or may give to one creditor security for the payment of his demand in preference to another" is the first touchstone. The debtor, absent fraud, does not have to treat creditors fairly. The second touchstone is "in the absence of fraud, every contract of a debtor is valid against all his creditors, existing or subsequent, who have not acquired a lien on the property affected by such contract." Whether embodied in local state statute or common law (dating back to King Henry II, probably), this is the state of the law. Article 9 (secured transactions) of the Uniform Commercial Code grants priority to secured creditors over unsecured creditors, and this is the third touchstone.

The sly trick that a third party (usually a credit manager's association) can take involves a blanket lien (a filed UCC financing statement) taken on behalf of the alleged consenting creditors, which effectively immunizes the debtor's assets from enforcement by the alleged non consenting creditors. In the event of a levy upon the debtor's bank account, the third party would file a third party claim, which seeks to dissolve the levy based on the credit manager's pre-existing lien and shelter the bank account from the creditor's enforcement. A alleged "consenting creditor," of course, would refrain from the filing of suit. The end result is that one group of creditors, who are willing to accept payments, ousts (through an intermediary) non consenting creditors, eliminating their access to the debtor's assets. If the debtor, through its surrogate (the credit manager's association) ousts the dissident creditors, the debtor has engineered a de facto stay imposed upon the non consenting creditors, immunity from enforcement, a long term payment program, and unfettered control over assets without court supervision. Of course, the "consenting creditor" and "non consenting creditor" is a total fiction. The intermediary is claiming the existence of these creditors, but by in large, these creditors do not exist.

When Do I File a Claim?

The debtor (or representative) arbitrarily sets forth the date upon which the creditor must accept or reject this offer. If you want to accept the offer, accept sooner than later. Sometimes the debtor or the debtor's agent imposes ridiculously short time frames to accept or reject an offer.

What Does It Mean to File a Claim?

Use personal delivery, overnight services, USPS Express mail, and maybe fax. Email is uncertain, but you can try.

How Do I Locate the Offer?

First, call the debtor or the debtor's attorney or agent. The debtor, through an attorney or agent or even itself, might communicate an offer. This is the Wild West. If a debtor wants you to accept ten cents on the dollar, trust me: He or she will put this offer in front of you.

What Do I File?

Typically, the debtor (through the intermediary) proffers (or demands) their own form of claim or acceptance, including "sign here on the dotted line." These offers are tricky and intentionally so. The acceptance of the offer is more than just agreeing to accept pennies on the dollar. The acceptance also compels the creditor to release the guarantors; release the collateral; and issue a global release of all liability, including claims against a surety, bonding company, alter ego, or legitimate third party. The creditor will be releasing the kitchen sink. Be wary of any deal that states words to the effect that the "terms and conditions" of this agreement are set forth in such and such document, which you might not have at hand. This is an immediate tip-off of trouble.

Do I Get Accruing Interest?

No. Interest stops per the agreement you sign, unless otherwise allowed. Workout deals seek to stop the accrual of interest, even if the claim is secured.

Do I Need to Update the Claim?

Yes, you should, if, for example, the debt is increased by bounced checks, credits that have been disallowed, or other changes.

Who Gets the Claim?

The debtor, the debtor's attorney, and the intermediary. Read the claim form more than once. This is one of these "no kidding moments" here. Debtors, their attorneys, and their agents intend to make everything as complicated as possible to burden the creditor.

What Should I Include?

Everything. However, these workouts are offers by the debtor, which the creditor might accept by signing an acceptance, or filing a claim, or some other act of agreement. These deals do not compel the debtor to pay. The debtor can literally ignore deal.

Are There Privacy Issues?

Redact social security numbers, driver's license numbers, bank account numbers, and other clearly private information.

What Should I Expect from the Court and Other Parties?

Don't expect anything—even an acknowledgment of your claim. Confirm receipt. Absent someone pushing the debtor into an involuntary bankruptcy, there is no court supervision. These are private deals between the debtor and the creditors. Sometimes they work and sometimes they flop. Don't expect the court to "drop from the sky" to straighten out some misunderstanding, error, or the misdeeds of the debtor.

Is There Judicial Supervision?

No, none, and there probably never will be.

Is There a Risk of Side Deals?

Guaranteed. The purpose of these deals is usually to hide some side deal that looted the company, embezzlement, or creation of a new entity, while the original entity dies on the vine or just defaults. However, sometimes these deals pan out and creditors get a better deal than is available through a bankruptcy, assignment, or even bulk sale.

Are There Statutory Safeguards against Fraud?

None. This is the Wild West. Each creditor, when offered a fraction of the debt, makes his or her own decision based on the amount of the debt; the offer; the cost of collection; the success of any collection or suit activities; the likelihood that the debtor might file bankruptcy anyway; and the amount of time, effort, and energy that might be expended to follow the collection case to the bitter end.

Can Another Party Object to My Claim?

Who knows? This is a completely opaque arrangement. Not too likely, but you never know. The debtor is control of the process. A claim that is bad (i.e., fraudulent) is probably filed by the debtor's surrogate.

If There Is an Objection, What Happens?

Unclear and unknown.

What Does the Debtor or Intermediary Provide at Close?

Maybe a summary accounting and maybe nothing at all. The debtor and its intermediary do not bear any real duty to the creditors. The creditors might well claim that the intermediary is their agent, but the intermediary will claim that the intermediary is the debtor's agent (potentially correct), or an escrow holder (potentially correct), or maybe the creditor's agent (potentially correct, given the filing of the UCC financing statement with the secretary of state). Your expectations are in the basement here. This is not a judicial enterprise, but a private deal between the parties. Sometimes these deals are opaque because the debtor or cohorts looted the bank accounts, among other assets, and nobody, but nobody, is willing to sign their name to an accounting.

What Are the Priorities?

Unknown and unclear because the debtor remains in charge. The debtor can direct the intermediary to pay whomever the debtor directs, even in contravention with the claim forms. The debtor will assert that the debtor retains control of its cash and can spend it anyway it wishes. Absent extenuating events, few creditors (more likely, no one) would finance very sophisticated litigation to unwind these deals or get an injunction, which is even more expensive.

Do I Have a Right to Object to Another Claim?

It is nearly impossible.

When Can I Object?

Not likely and not ever.

Do I Have Remedies if a Bad Claim Has Been Filed?

None. The debtor can pay whomever the debtor chooses. Depending upon the terms of the claim, you might have waived your right to sue the third party for a fraudulent conveyance or illegal payment (e.g., payment to an insider that is an unlawful corporate distribution).

What About Accuracy of Claims and Liability?

The claim form is probably under penalty of perjury, which is the standard ploy to coerce creditors to file an honest claim. Forcing someone to swear their life away is "chest beating" in debtor and creditor relations.

Is Compliance with FDCPA Required?

Probably. This includes an entire body of federal and state consumer protection law, assuming the debts are consumer. This is terribly unlikely but not impossible.

When Do I See an Accounting or Money?

Whenever the debtor pays and whenever the money is distributed. You see money on a monthly or quarterly basis if it works out. Maybe, but do not count on it.

When Should I Expect Payment?

When and if money is ever paid. The intermediary takes its share (10% to 15%) and likewise reimburses itself for costs and fees due its attorneys. Furthermore, the intermediary pockets the interest.

How Is Transparency?

Poor to downright nonexistent.

What Are Some Other Options?

An involuntary bankruptcy or receivership.

Stay of Legal Proceedings?

Depends on the terms of the offer. Count on a contractual stay of any proceedings against the debtor or third parties should you agree to a long term payment agreement. Remember, these deals are concocted by the folks whose goal is to deter creditors from taking any legal action. Expect language in a workout that prevents creditors from filing suit.

Guarantor Status?

This is a total bomb. Absent a waiver, these payment programs would exonerate the guarantor based on the alteration of the debt. Worse, the claim form probably provides for a broad discharge. Enormous care is required to insure that the personal guaranty survives these deals.

Overall Fairness?

Some of these deals are acceptable. Whether you are getting a fair or decent deal is left to the "kindness of strangers."

Right to Declare an Exemption?

Maybe.

Right of Reclamation?

Count on the waiver in the claim form to discharge the rights of reclamation under Section 2702, which permits a creditor to claim goods sold within 10 days to an insolvent and further back if there is a misrepresentation in writing. Assume that the goods are long gone and turned into cash, which vitiates the reclamation claim. However, make the demand for reclamation anyway. The enemy here is the third party who is going to claim a "security interest" in all of the debtor's property, which might include all goods sold on the cusp of the insolvency. What does this mean in English? This means that the intermediary, who is the debtor's agent and surrogate, is going to claim status as a secured creditor for the benefit of "consenting creditors." This "secured creditor" (who is actually the debtor's agent) will claim that the goods subject to reclamation are subordinate to the perfected security interest. Does this sound bad? You bet. This is terrible because the debtor can immune the goods subject to a valid reclamation right through the ruse of a security interest by the intermediary.

What Are My Proactive Strategies?

The creditor can seek a pre-judgment writ of attach that might encumber the assets that entitled the non consenting to priority and secured status. Many credit applications, loan documents, and other papers offer the creditor secured status, but a financing statement might, or might not, have been filed or been filed properly. File the UCC if possible. Pursue all rights of reclamation. Pursue all rights to put the debtor on creditor hold based on reasonable insecurity of performance (UCC Code Section 2609). An involuntary bankruptcy might unwind the security interest, but the involuntary must be filed within 90 days of the security interest. If you have money to invest and feel strongly that this workout is a total ruse (likely but not for sure), you can file suit to stop this transaction, seek the appointment of a receiver, or seek to impound all funds under an attachment on the grounds the transaction is fraudulent conveyance. The whole purpose of this workout, and the security interest, is that the debtor seeks to hide assets, conceal funds, or pay creditors pennies on the dollar, for no reason at all. This is a classic fraudulent conveyance because the debtor is transferring its assets to a third party (its surrogate) with the intention to hinder, delay, and defraud other creditors.

The Long Story

What Is a Workout?

A workout is an arrangement to pay off a past due debt. Nobody wants to be sued. Nobody wants to send a matter to collection. Nobody wants to hire an attorney. Every vendor, bank, leasing company, and landlord wants to get paid debt with the least effort, time, and expense. Most debtors want to retire a bushel of past due debt, but stay in business and even maintain good relations with key vendors. A maxim of business is pay key vendors who supply the core products to a business, lest the key vendor pull the plug on the business, which goes down the drain.

Workouts are common. A customer runs up a debt. Facing collection, the customer offers to make installment payments over a year. Is this a good deal? Yes and no. Yes; this is a great deal if the customer pays on time because suing the customer will accrue fees and expenses. No; this is a bad deal because the creditor, typically a wholesale vendor, wants payment immediately because the creditor has to pay its bills on time. Creditors reject "vendor financing." Sometimes, and more times than not, chest beating gets the debtor to pay up. Some vendors relish the reputation of a tough guy, which prompts customers to pay on time.

Workouts consist of a payment program, which means that the debtor promises to pay the debt over a period of time. The debtor can agree verbally, enter into a formal workout agreement, or even sign a promissory note. Sometimes the debtor owes the butcher, baker, and candlestick maker. This is more often than not—if the debtor owes one creditor, the debtor owes many creditors.

Some creditors are more aggressive than others. The IRS and state taxing authorities proceed based on their playbook, which means that they will lien and levy the debtor. The debtor might have defaulted on the business lease and personal property leases for key business equipment, and face collection calls from agencies and attorneys.

Risks

What is wrong with workouts? The debtor defaults because the debtor is overwhelmed, runs out of money, or decides to file bankruptcy (Chapter 13). Another creditor suffers from "ants in the pants" and levies the debtor's bank account, which causes the debtor's checks to bounce. Some debtors use the payment program to let the statute of limitation pass for bankruptcy preferences and fraudulent conveyance actions. Once the statute has run out, the debtor files a bankruptcy in which the trustee is hobbled in bringing these actions. Some debtors have crappy books—or no books. They have no idea how much they owe or to whom. Anecdotal but helpful here is the all too common story of a commercial debtor coming to see a bankruptcy attorney. When asked about accounting records, the debtor hands over a bag of unopened mail, which consists of collection letters, dunning notices, and lawsuits. The debtor has no idea of the extent of its liabilities. Working is out is cheap because the debtor does not need complete sworn bankruptcy schedules, which require some accounting support. (However, when bankruptcy schedules list "unknown" for every creditor, chances are good the debtor has no records.)

The major risk of a workout is that the debtor will liquidate any remaining assets (including emptying out the bank account) and precipitously file a no asset Chapter 7. This is very bad because the debtor can empty everything of value by paying key creditors (who might be family members) or, alternatively, by converting non exempt funds into exempt assets.

Varieties

Workouts come in many varieties. The usual are extensions, which is a fancy word for a payment agreement; a cash compromise (50 cents on the dollar—take it or leave it); a pot plan, which is a percentage paid to each creditor from a fixed sum of money; or an earn-out, which is a promise of payment from the debtor's (or successor's) gross or net profits.

Some workouts enable the debtor to retire past due debt and return to financial health. Some workouts are a dead man walking because the debtor is actually broke. The debtor will make the first payment and drop dead in days.

What Is an Extension Plan?

An extension plan enables the debtor to make periodic payments to satisfy the debtor, either in full or in part. If the debtor owes $24,000.00, the debtor offers to pay the debt at $1,000 a month for 24 months. Extension programs are the stable of all credit professionals. The key points are the following:

1. Confirm the balance due and ratify the debt and re-start the statute of limitations. Ratify all agreements, including the sales agreement, contracts, terms and conditions, warranties, the credit agreement, and personal guaranties.
2. Impose a firm start date for payment.

3. Set a rate of interest but be mindful whether usury applies (or does not apply). Add penalties for nonpayment of an installment when due. If interest or penalties are unpaid, they are added to the principal, which increased amount is subject to new accruing interest and penalties. A default in payment might even increase the rate of interest on a permanent basis. Consider compounding of interest but check with local state law.

4. Provide for specific dates when the payments are due. Attach the payment schedule to avoid any doubt when payments are due.

5. Specify place where payments are to made.

6. Apply payments first to accruing interest and balance to principal.

7. Payments are due on the first, with five days grace thereafter. Grace or notice is not required by state law, but an expectation of the debtor.

8. Three written notices of default in which the debtor has another five days to cure the default. The parties should spell out the email, physical mail address, or fax number that would be the recipient of any written notice.

9. In the event that the debtor fails to cure the default, or exhaustion of the three notice of grace, the creditor may, at its option, and without notice, accelerate the remaining installments, declare the same due and payable and proceed to enforce all rights and remedies.

10. Venue (place of suit) is the place of business of the creditor because the contract recites that the place of contracting is the creditor's locale.

11. The contract has a forum selection clause at the place of business of the creditor, but at the creditor's option to file in the forum where the debtor maintains its place of business.

12. Choice of law is the law where the creditor has its main office.

13. Double check the sale agreement, credit application or contract, or terms and conditions on the invoices, which likewise might spell out a factual basis for venue, form selection, and choice of law.

14. In the event of enforcement of the contract, the creditor is entitled to reasonable attorney's fees and court costs.

15. Be sure the contract has been ratified and approved by the guarantor, if any, and that the contract for an extension does not waive, exonerate, or discharge the guarantor. Alternatively, the

principals of the debtor guaranty the liability of the debtor under the contract for the extension.

16. The contract incorporates a broad based security interest in the assets of the debtor, which includes all now owned and hereinafter acquired assets and potentially a deed of trust or mortgage encumbering the debtor's real property. This is very important because per se the debtor is insolvent and subject to other potential liens, levies, and mortgages that might encumber the debtor's property and diminish any recovery in the event of a liquidation of the debtor's assets.

17. The contract provides that the creditor can accept a non conforming tender without a waiver of the right to demand and receive, and declare a default, if the event of a default by any subsequently non conforming tender or default.

18. All payments are by wire transfer and not the mails.

19. Before entering into this deal, run the debtor through PACER (the U.S. Courts) to determine if the debtor has filed bankruptcy, the state courts to determine if the debtor is the subject to one or more lawsuits, the county recorder to locate other liens, and obtain from the debtor a sworn financial statement.

20. Expect that the debtor might default. Few debtors survive the rigors of a long term payment program. In light of the risk of default, some creditors demand a very large down payment (about 50%) on the basis that the initial big investment compels the debtor to continue the payments to reap the benefit of the payment program, which discharges the debt.

21. Aside from nonpayment of an installment, the payment contract should permit an immediate acceleration of the remaining installment in the event of bulk sale, sale, transfer of any assets outside the ordinary course of business, or any act that would make the creditor reasonably insecure of the debtor's continuing performance.

Any payment program bears risk because the debtor has already run into the financial trouble that necessitated the payment contract. Absent some miraculous rehabilitation, most extensions sputter and die a painful death.

A payment program should be consistent with, or at least mindful of, the contract, sale agreement, credit application, terms and conditions on the invoice or statement, or online terms to insure consistency and avoid waiver. Most major customers (department stores, national food chains, etc.) now post online their vendor terms and conditions.

Workouts, loan rollovers, and rewrites are a common practicing in finance, which includes traditional banking, hard money lending, and other variations. The simplest workout is that the borrower borrows $1,000,000 on a five term loan, but with an amortization of a 30 year loan at 5%. The monthly payment is $5,368.22, but the loan is due in 60 months. Assuming a start date of April 1, 2015, and maturity of April 1, 2020, the balloon will be $916,745.30. This loan is a good deal for the borrower because the borrower has access to unrestricted cash of $1,000,000 and bears low dollar payments. If the debtor can invest the $1,000,000 in inventory with a 20% net profit, which turns over 30 times (6 times a year) during the five years, at a cost of $5,368.22, the debtor makes a killing. When the loan comes due, and assuming that the debtor paid the installments on time, the debtor would seek a rollover from the financial institution.

In commercial roll-overs and forbearance transactions, most lenders demand that the borrower release the lender of any liability (i.e., execute a release of all claims against the lender). This is an expectation of every transaction. The wording starts something like the following: "Borrower releases lender of any claims, cause of action, choses in action, rights of action, claims of loss, liability or damage, whether in tort, contract, or violation of law, statute, rule or regulations, whether known or unknown . . ." Standard releases consume pages. Expect reaffirmation of the debt, a jury trial waiver, agreement to reference (private judge under the auspices of the court), forum selection, choice of law, factual for venue, aggregation of total debt (including accrued interest into a new principal which itself accrues interest), and access to all financial records. This is the short list. These are key terms that have significance in the event of default. This is more than just "boilerplate," but rather a waiver by the borrower.

What Is an Earn-Out?

Another variation of the payment program is that the debtor pays to the creditor, or a creditor representative on behalf of many creditors, a percentage of gross or net revenues until the debt is paid in full or until a percentage of the debt is paid. The money due the creditor is somewhat contingent upon the success of the debtor and, more likely, the successor to the debtor.

In some cases, the debtor transfers its assets to a new entity (e.g., "NewCo"), which assumes the debts (or some of the debts) and agrees to liquidate the debts based on a percentage of net or gross profits (i.e., the "earn-out"). Many attempt this trick, but few succeed. These earn-outs might bear the same name, host the same management, and sell the same product or services, but they face the same marketing and capital challenges as the predecessor.

While some earn-outs are successful, many run into trouble because the creditors cannot tell if the debtor (or the third party agent) is remitting the correct percentage of gross or net profits. In other cases, the debtor manipulates its records to eliminate any sign of gross or net profits. In many instances, the debtor creates another entity, transfers its assets to the new entity, and claims that the original entity ("OldCo") went out of business, which forecloses any continuing payments. Absent a fraudulent conveyance action or other action to impose liability under the successor, NewCo might well skate. This is not to say that legal recourse would be futile. This is to say that legal recourse is expensive, and someone has to foot the bill. Rest assured that the transfer from OldCo to NewCo is exceedingly common, propelled by "debtor fatigue."

Temptation looms very large to weasel out of the earn-out. This risk of a fraudulent conveyance compels the creditor (or creditors) to demand a perfected security interest and personal guaranty. Somebody has got to be very adroit and alert here.

Creditor trade associations, including credit manager's associations, independent insolvency agents, assignees, receivers, and bankruptcy trustees act as disbursement agents on behalf of the debtor in payment to claimants. The debt "servicers" are not cheap, but they are useful in managing the payments. They remind the debtor to make a payment when past due. Expect that the debtor will grant a blanket security interest in favor of the disbursing agents to "secure" payment under the agreement. This security is bogus and a fraudulent conveyance because in the event of default the debtor has the right to rescind the security interest.

Let me repeat one theme for the reader: Everyone is clever. Everyone is smart. Everyone has or will execute a strategy here. From the viewpoint of the creditor, and particularly a large creditor who can afford counsel, the trick is to expect the marching band—lots of folks coming and going with their own schemes.

What Is a Pot Plan?

No, this is not a business plan to sell marijuana nor a story about pots and pans. No Cooking Channel here. This is a plot to pay creditors a percentage from a fixed sum of money. I quote from a recent letter: "unsecured claims will aggregate approximately $120,000.00 . . . it [the debtor] will have approximately $20,000 [from liquidation of assets] available for distribution to creditors." This is a pot plan.

A pot plan comes in two varieties. The usual is that the debtor marshals a sum of money that is paid to the creditors on a pro rata basis in full satisfaction of the debt. For instance, the pot is $10,000.00 and claims are $100,000.00, so the creditors recover 10% on the dollar. Pot plans are very old and well understood.

A creditor is not obligated to accept the offer. If a creditor declines the offer, the creditor can sue, serve, get a judgment, and execute. If the "pot" consisted of the liquidation proceeds of the debt, the judgment creditor would recover nothing. The judgment creditor might be a tad upset, but generally a debtor has the right to prefer one creditor over another. This right to prefer means, absent some fraud, that the payment by the debtor to another creditor is final, even though other creditors are left out in the cold.

Of course, upon the announcement of the pot plan, the creditor can seek an ex parte writ of attachment that might enable the creditor to reach the "pot." This is an uncertainty. The pot ostensibly is the property of the debtor and, therefore, like any other assets, it is subject to an attachment. The countervailing claim is that the pot is held in trust for the benefit of the creditor who accepts, and that the debtor has forfeited title. In reaching the pot, the creditor would have to prove that the debtor controlled distribution of the funds. "Control" means that the debtor implicitly has the right to recall or cancel the "pot" and retrieve the funds. The right of recall means that the debtor still owns the pot, which a creditor can attach. Pot plans raise lots of questions. If the debtor's property, which was liquidated to create the pot, was subject to a valid security interest, the "pot" constitutes proceeds under the security interest that should remitted to the secured party and not to the general unsecured creditors. Other parties might have an interest in the debtor's assets or proceeds. The usual suspects are judgment creditors holding valid judgment liens and attachment liens and tax authorities who have liens or a statutory priority in any liquidation of the debtor's assets. Wage claimants, family law creditors, and consumers might have a priority claim. These competing claims poison the pot and reduce any real recovery due the creditors, or worse, drain the pot entirely.

Another pot plan variation is that the debtor agrees to pay a fixed percentage without regard to the amount at hand (what is in the pot) or the total of the creditors who accept (or reject) the plan.

Absent a clear waiver in the personal guaranty, acceptance of payment from a pot plan in satisfaction of the debt will probably exonerate the guarantor under a personal guaranty. This is a very big deal, particularly if the guarantor is financially capable of paying the total due under the guaranty. Most commercial guaranties entitle the creditor to accept less than the full amount from the debtor and proceed against the guaranty, but all guaranties are strictly construed against the creditor. All preprinted forms are construed against the creditor. All ambiguities are construed against the drafter, who is always the creditor. The issue of exoneration is a big deal if, for example, the debt is $100,000.00 and the distribution from the pot is $10,000.00. The creditor most assuredly would like to collect the $90,000 from the guarantor, particularly if the guarantor is solvent.

The simplest workout is the debtor pays a discounted amount in full payment of the debt. Some creditors willingly accept 75% on the dollar given that the collection agency or attorney fees are about 25% anyway. If the debtor is financially distressed, or headed to bankruptcy court, many creditors readily take 25% on the dollar if the money is paid promptly. If the debt is under $20,000.00, and the creditor is large commercial institution, settlements are common. The exceptions are banks, who loath discounted settlement for fear that too many customers will manufacture a phony excuse that justifies pennies on the dollar. Routinely, business people falling on hard times offer "pennies on the dollar," including very famous business people who are New York developers.

How Fair Are Workouts?

Workouts are opaque. The debtor is making an offer to pay creditors that the creditors can accept or reject. The business judgment for the creditor is whether the offer, and absolute performance, are a good deal under the circumstances (i.e., amount of debt; financial condition of the debtor; cost of collection litigation; likelihood of recovery; risk of bankruptcy; amount of time, effort, and energy of the creditor). In many cases, the debtor and creditors engage in bargaining, which can increase the recovery to the creditors (i.e., don't take the first offer). These offers are not so bad because the creditor might collect without accruing a third party expense or collection fee.

The creditor faces additional considerations: The amount owed to the creditor might be modest, compelling the creditor to consider a quick settlement. The sale to the debtor might have been troubled at the outset because the creditor failed to secure a personal guaranty, an EFT agreement, or other assurances of payment. The workout might provide for immediate payment, which, even if 50% on the dollar or less, is better than waiting years if the debtor files bankruptcy.

Collection "politics" comes into play. While the principals of the debtor might have looted the company or offered phony financials to convince the creditor to accept pennies on the dollar, few creditors are willing to invest big money to chase down the debtor if the debtor is offering something of value at the outset. Spending real money to collect a written off bad debt is a tough call because the collection of debts is unpredictable, chaotic, and the expense train never stops.

Commercial vendors are sophisticated credit grantors. They believe in the motto that the "first loss is the best loss," and the ensuing motto, "cut your losses when you can." Collection agencies and collection attorneys charge anywhere between 15% to 50% on the dollar. Any recovery that approaches the net recovery after hiring a third party professional is a fair recovery. A commercial creditor wants the collection process to work, but doesn't want to be a victim of the collection process.

The answer to whether a workout is fair or unfair is in the eyes of the beholder—and in that beholder's desire to resolve the matter quickly or prolong the quest. Most workouts are fair if the creditor is paid a substantial portion of the debt without the necessity of third party expenses. If the creditor is paid 50% from a pot plan, or cash discount at once, the creditor might be satisfied. On the other hand, some workouts are unfair because the debtor engages in pyrotechnics to bamboozle the creditor to accept pennies on the dollar when the debtor is, in fact, solvent or could pay a greater percentage. Some creditors walk away from a workout convinced that the debtor hoodwinked everyone. Some creditors are just obstinate and want to litigate.

The next chapter explains receiverships. Receiverships are very old remedies, but they rarely create the arena of traditional debtor and creditor conflict. Receivers are usually the agent of a party who seeks to capture property of the debtor, which the receiver would manage, administer, and even sell. Call the receiver the court's right hand person, who fulfills the court mandate to protect and preserve real and personal property. Generally, creditors are a stranger in the land of receivers.

14

Receiverships

The Short Story

Synopsis

Receivers are no friend to the creditors of the underlying debtor. Courts appoint receivers at the behest of a specific aggrieved party to take possession of the debtor's property usually for the purpose of satisfying the aggrieved party's claim or interest. For example, courts appoint receivers to preside over partnership disputes, corporate dissolutions, family law proceedings, or other matters that require a third party to liquidate assets and distribute proceedings.

Sometimes, receivers do appear in the prosecution of pre- and post-judgment remedies on behalf of creditors. These receivers are appointed by the court to liquidate a debtor's property for the benefit of the specific creditor at hand. These receivers are relatively rare given their significant expense and the fact that the creditor can execute upon the debtor's property. In the enforcement of a judgment, a receiver is required to liquidate the debtor's interest in a liquor license, patent, trademark, copyright, domain name, and other intellectual property. Receivers might serve the interest of a creditor in collecting large-scale portfolios of receivables.

The most common receivers are sought by banks, financiers, and hard money lenders who seek to foreclose upon real property. This real property is more than just raw land, but includes apartment buildings, commercial properties, industrial properties, farms, developments, hotels, hospitals, and other health facilities. These receivers are necessary to operate the businesses attached to the real property, not only for the benefit of the secured party and to avoid waste, but for the protection of all parties concerned to avoid any risk of personal injury, damage, vandalism to the property, or other calamity. A secured creditor might seek to appoint a receiver to recover personal property collateral, including intellectual property, inventory, equipment, furniture, fixtures, furnishings, and the like. Such a receiver would take possession of this collateral and arrange for an orderly sale, possibly as a going business. Any collection by a receiver would be remitted to the secured party after judicial approval and an accounting. The IRS and Securities & Exchange Commission routinely seek the appointment of a receiver pending the outcome of an enforcement or regulatory action.

State Attorney Generals likewise seek receivers similarly for enforcement or regulatory actions. This list is illustrative, not exhaustive.

A debtor might stipulate to the appointment of a receiver, but will almost never actually seek the appointment of a receiver to operate its business in the face of insolvency. In the event of insolvency, nearly every debtor will exercise its rights under the Bankruptcy Code, or pursue a non-bankruptcy alternative, such as an assignment, bulk sale, or voluntary workout. Receivers are by and large an adjunct to the court engaged to properly care for and maintain a specific asset for the benefit of a specific party. Obviously, from time to time, the receivership estate might generate sufficient funds to be applied to the claims of creditors, but this is unusual.

Legal Basis

Receivership came from English Common Law. Proportional distribution to creditors originated in the English Bankruptcy Act of 1542. Federal law (FRCP 66) and every state authorizes the appointment of a receivership. The U.S. Internal Revenue Code and the Securities and Exchange Commission statutes, among many others, authorize the appointment of a receiver. The court has the right under common law to appoint a receiver separate and apart from FRCP 66 and/or state law.

A receiver is a creature of equity, which authorizes the court to appoint a receiver. Most post-judgment enforcement statutes authorize a judge to appoint a receiver in aid of enforcement. Depending upon the exigency, some judges demand an exhaustion of other remedies before appointing a receiver. A court may appoint a receiver based upon exigent circumstances, which tend to arise out of the operation of a business, including, but not limited to, an apartment building, hotel, agricultural property, commercial property, or retail store, particularly if the owner (i.e., the debtor) is unable, unwilling, or incapable of managing the business.

As a direct agent and officer of the court, the receiver takes legal title to the receivership estate for the purpose of administration. This is a moment for pause. The receiver takes "receiver's title" to the debtor's property to the extent that the receiver, subject to an order of the court, has the legal right to sell, lease, dispose, encumber, transfer, assign, liquidate, or abandon the property of the debtor. Upon the order of the court, a receiver can sign the debtor's name to a contract, deed, note, bill, transfer agreement, or even endorse the debtor's name to checks, drafts, or money orders. The receiver can open up a bank account in the name of the debtor, but the receiver would be the signatory.

When Do I File a Claim?

Receivers typically do not acknowledge receipt of a creditor's claim because a receiver, unless ordered by a court, does not act in a trustee capacity on behalf of the creditors nor would the receiver distribute any of the profits and proceeds of the receivership to the creditors. Sometimes, a receiver might have the role of a trustee on behalf of creditors. In fact, many receiverships safeguard, manage, and liquidate property. Typically, the proceeds from a receivership are due the secured creditor who sought the appointment, partners in the midst of a partnership dispute, creditors or shareholders in a corporate dissolution, or the government as part of the statute that authorized the appointment of a receiver.

The order appointing the receiver might (or, more likely, might not) provide for payment of general unsecured claims. This creates an oddball situation in which the court order did not authorize the receiver to entertain payment of general unsecured claims. Many receivers do not even acknowledge receipt of a general unsecured claim. Sometimes, a receiver might enjoy a surplus estate, which means that the receiver generated funds over and above what is due to the secured creditor. While years ago, this was a rare instance, a hyper-inflated real estate market might produce buyers who would pay more than the balance due on secured loans, therefore leading to a surplus estate. Should this event occur, the unsecured creditor might be able to intervene in the receivership action, subject to a court order, and assuming a viable claim or interest, oppose the motion filed by the receiver to distribute funds or assets. Assuming a viable claim against the debtor, and that the estate is solvent, the receiver can move to intervene in the receivership estate, and, if granted, seek an order compelling the receiver to pay the excess process to the creditor based upon the creditor's claim against the debtor.

What Does It Mean to File a Claim (if Possible)?

Assuming that the receiver will accept claims of creditors, as authorized by the court order, and based on the mandate of the order, timing is critical because the order provides for probably 30 to 90 days to file a claim. Reliable overnight or other express mail is a requirement. Personal delivery also is viable. The creditor is 100% responsible for familiarizing himself/herself with the contents of the receivership order. Judges have no patience for a creditor who missed a bar date, absent the most extraordinary circumstances.

How Do I Locate Information?

Receivers do not send out notice to creditors, absent a court order. Receivers typically do not publish the receivership order in a newspaper or online. Receivers typically do not inform the general public that they are running a business, unless required. In many cases, creditors only learn about a receivership when they contact the debtor, or the person running the debtor's business, who tells them that the debtor's business is in a receivership. If the creditor is lucky, the debtor or third party will send by email the receivership order.

What Do I File?

Assuming that you can file a claim, you might have to file a claim with the court on pleading paper, specifying the amount, basis, total due, support documentation, and accruing interest (the rate and daily amount). This is another moment of pause. A receiver, by virtue of his or her appointment, takes custody of the property subject to all prior liens and encumbrances, even if fraudulent, overstated, incorrect, or otherwise. A receiver cannot "strip liens and encumbrances" like a bankruptcy trustee could do. A receiver can never sell property "free and clear" absent an order in which everybody consents. A junior secured creditor is well advised to inform the receiver of the position of the secured creditor, engage an attorney, and file a motion to intervene to make sure that the junior secured creditor is paid from the proceeds of any sale.

Do I Get Accruing Interest?

Yes, for secured claims, including the secured claim of the creditor who initiated the case. A junior secured creditor is entitled to interest, if there is equity for the junior secured creditor.

Yes, for unsecured claims if the estate is solvent. No, for unsecured claims if the estate is insolvent.

Do I Need to Update the Claim?

Yes, but rarely does a receiver pay claims. The answer to this question really applies to the senior and junior secured creditors; they are obligated to update the accrual of interest, costs, and attorneys' fees. This must be done.

Who Gets the Claim?

Well, filing a claim and serving all of these folks might be a complete non-starter. Before papering everybody to death, the receiver has to examine the receivership order, and absent a provision for unsecured creditors, file a motion to intervene in order to assert the claim, and likewise determine if the receivership would provide for payment of junior secured claims or unsecured creditors.

Assuming that the creditor passes this milestone, file the proof of claim with the court, the receiver, the receiver's attorney, the debtor, the debtor's attorney, and everyone else remotely connected with the case. Service requirements are a big deal and require a lot of time, money and effort.

What Should I Include?

Everything. This means a copy, not the original, of all documentation, proof of the security, payment stream and calculation, and any written promises of payment.

Are There Privacy Issues?

Redact social security numbers, driver's license numbers, bank account numbers, and other clearly private information. Take this seriously. Why get sued over an FDCPA infraction (or an infraction of a dozen other consumer bodies of law)?

What Should I Expect from the Receiver (and When)?

Not much. Confirm receipt. Check the order. Again, you might expect something from the receiver only if the receiver is responsible for the payment of creditors' claims.

Is There Judicial Supervision?

Yes, for all conduct of the receiver, post-appointment, based on the tenure of the order. The state and local rules of the court apply; the particular judge might impose his or her own rules, requirements for accounting and disclosures, and reimbursements of fees and costs. Associations of receivership offer their own handbooks, which are helpful. Very closely aligned to a receiver are professional fiduciaries that have to be licensed and bonded and subject to their own rule. Professional receivers seek approval for any transaction. Nearly all judges are fastidious in their management of receiverships.

Is There a Risk of Side Deals?

Yes, a very high one, prior to the appointment of the receiver. Unlike bankruptcy, which compels disclosures and enables the trustee to "reach back" to recover hidden or transferred assets, the receivership estate lacks these powers. Post appointment, the receiver is the agent of the court.

Consider a receiver the helmsman of a sinking ship. Ships do not sink without warning. Ships take on water, list 30 degrees to the port side, some of the deck hands go overboard, and the survivors get into the life boats. This will take some time. Rest assured that during these moments of chaos, some insiders are looking hither and yon for something to float away on.

Are There Statutory Safeguards against Fraud?

Prior to the appointment of a receiver, there are none. Post appointment, the court supervises the receiver. Depending the vicissitudes of the order appointing the receiver, the receiver needs the judicial hall pass to visit the bathroom.

Can Another Party Object to My Claim?

Depending upon the order and the local rules of court, and whether the receivership anticipates claims from unsecured creditors, the answer is uncertain. The receiver is in charge. If somebody files a bogus claim, the aggrieved creditor should make a demand upon the receiver to reject the claim and litigate it.

Absent the cooperation of the receiver or the depth and skill of an experienced attorney, the objecting creditor would have to make a full fledged showing that the errant claim is bad and that the receiver is doing nothing about it.

If There Is an Objection, What Happens?

If the estate produces sufficient funds to creditors, the receiver's objection to a claim would necessitate a full frontal response, akin to a very well pled and detailed complaint.

Likewise, a creditor could object to the claim, which would initiate nothing less than high stakes litigation. Typically, claims objections arise upon the filing of inflated claims by insiders or the cronies of the debtor.

What Does the Receiver Provide at Close?

The receiver files a motion to approve the accounting of receipts and disbursements and to seek ratification of the receiver's performance, disbursement of funds on hand, exoneration of the bond, and discharge. Depending upon local rules and the order, the receivers provide detailed accountings. If the court grants this motion, the receiver is discharged of liability to all parties, including creditors, assuming notice.

What Are the Priorities?

Receivers take possession of property in distress. In English, this means that the owner neglected management, maintenance, payment of key vendors, payment of utilities, payment of accounting services, personal services, day-to-day debts and services, property taxes, or other key expenses. Receivers pay these ongoing expenses—and prior expenses, if necessary—to maintain the property, including key vendors, employees, the landlord, utilities, insurance, and other core expenses. The party appointing a receiver has to finance all of these expenses. If these expenses are not paid, they have the right of priority of payment from the proceeds. The court likewise would order payment of these expenses if arising during the administration of the case. These expenses would also include charges for insurance, maintenance, taxes, administrative fees and charges, wages, workers' compensation charges, and other routine business expenses.

Depending upon the type of receivership (foreclosure of real property, operation of a business, dissolution of corporation or LLC, partnership wind-up, family law battle), the court orders payment to the party who sought the receivership in the first place, based upon their interest in the property. If it is a foreclosure or judgment enforcement, the court orders the receiver to pay the creditors who initiated the proceeding. If it is a dissolution, the court orders payment to the owners of the business. If it is a governmental receivership, the court orders payment to the government or to victims. Absent the order, state statute, or local rule, the receiver will not pay general unsecured creditors. If it is a solvent estate (which is possible, given rising real estate values), the creditors might have to petition the court for payment; otherwise excess proceeds might go back to the defendant (i.e., the debtor). Receiverships are NOT creditor friendly.

Do I Have an Obligation to Object to Another Claim?

Not likely because this is the receiver's job.

When Can I Object?

Maybe never. Depends upon what the receiver wants to do here.

Do I Have Remedies if a Bad Claim Has Been Filed?

Unknown. The receiver can ignore the claim, negotiate a settlement, or pay the claim. If you have standing, you might be able to object to the motion for a discharge and claim that the receiver wasted estate property in the payment of the bad claim. Or, if the receiver has sought authority to pay this allegedly bad claim, you can oppose the motion. Courts grant a receiver deference.

What About Accuracy of Claims and Liability?

Absent general state law on fraud and depending on the state, the filing of the claim is a privileged communication, which raises issues of immunity.

Is Compliance with FDCPA Required?

Probably, but still in flux. (This includes an entire body of federal and state consumer protection law.)

When Do I See an Accounting or Money?

Receivership might extend for months or even years. A party with a legal right to an accounting will receive one, as a receiver's accounting is required by law and an equitable mandate.

When Should I Expect Payment?

Maybe never—even more likely never if the receivership is for the benefit of the party appointing the receiver, and not the creditors. The assets of the receivership are in the receiver's care. Creditor specific receivers (receivers in aid of a foreclosure of a deed of trust, mortgage, or security interest) rarely generate funds for payment of general unsecured creditors.

How Is Transparency?

Nonexistent for conduct prior to the appointment unless part of the filings with the court. Post-appointment, and depending upon the order, judge, and local rules, transparency is good. Receiverships are public proceedings, and absent a sealing order, all the filings on the docket are public record.

What Are Some Other Options?

An involuntary bankruptcy—only if the property would generate money for unsecured creditors. A receiver lacks the power of a claw-back or the strong arm powers of a bankruptcy trustee. The receiver accepts the estate "as is" and is a lien creditor under Article 9 of the UCC, which enables the receiver to take priority over an unperfected and unsecured creditor.

Stay of Legal Proceedings?

A creditor cannot levy or execute upon the property, take any action to interfere with administration of the estate, or even sue the receiver without a prior court order. Depending upon the order and local state law, the creditor might be barred even from suing the debtor or related third parties. Check with the order and local law before taking any action. Taking action that is in contravention to any statutory or common law prohibition might constitute contempt of court.

Guarantor Status?

Depending upon the guaranty, the failure to file a claim in the receivership, assuming the right and availability of funds, might exonerate the guarantor based on the failure of the creditor to act diligently.

Overall Fairness?

Depending upon the order and local law, receivership can serve the interest of the parties who sought the appointment. While the receiver operates under the direction of the court, receivers are not repositories for the benefit of creditors, unless ordered. Many creditors learn that the assets of a debtor are in a receivership in which the party (e.g., the government, secured creditor, judgment creditor, partners, corporation or LLC dissolution) does not necessarily (or ever) provide for payment of creditors. The only candidates that realistically might offer payment of creditor claims are dissolutions of a corporation, partnership, or LLC, and only if provided by the order and mandated by statute.

Right to Declare an Exemption?

It depends on the case. If the receivership is sought in the enforcement of a money judgment, the debtor has the right to exempt property from enforcement. The fact of a receivership does not preclude the debtor from asserting exemption, but it does make exemptions more burdensome.

Right of Reclamation?

UCC Code Section 2702 permits a creditor to claim goods sold within 10 days to an insolvent and further back if there is a misrepresentation in writing. If the debtor turns the goods into cash (very likely), the creditor is an unsecured creditor, even though the subject of a fraud. Getting priority over the claims or interest of the plaintiff who sought the appointment of the receiver will taken enormous gymnastics. If the goods are resold and gone, the Section 2702 rights evaporate.

What Are My Proactive Strategies?

Given that title passes at the time that the receiver is appointed and posts a bond, or otherwise takes title to the assets, and depending upon the scope of the order, the creditor can seek a pre-judgment writ of attach that might encumber the assets that entitled the creditors to priority and secured status. Be careful to time your action to insure that you do not contravene the receiver's title and the receiver's court jurisdiction over the property. This maneuvering will take great diligence and effort in your attempt to encumber the property.

Should you succeed, you might have successfully asserted an interest in the receivership estate that entitles you to appear and participate in the proceedings and even seek payment—just junior to other lien holders. You will have standing to object to the receiver's sales, or other transactions, and even to oppose fees and the motion to exonerate the bond and discharge. Many credit applications, loan documents, and other papers offer the creditor secured status, but a financing statement might or might not have been filed, or filed properly, including a fixture filing. Unlike bankruptcies, which enable to trustee to unwind pre filing liens, levies, transfers, and other interests, a receiver might lack these powers and take the property subject to all liens, levies, and enforcement. However, "equity receivers" maintain the standing of a lien creditor under Article 9 of the UCC and therefore would take over unperfected and/or unsecured creditors.

The Long Story

What Is a Receiver?

A receiver is a person (a natural person or entity) appointed by a court to sell an asset, run a business, investigate some wrongdoing, take possession and hold property, or do some other act at the court's bidding. Consider a receiver the judicial "boots on the ground." The receiver is an agent of the court, and acts in the court's name and power. The receiver operates under the terms of the order appointing the receiver, and even under the court's equitable powers. The receiver is not a paid employee of the court, either party, or the government, although the court might appoint public administrators to act as conservators for individuals who are unable to manage their personal affairs. In nearly all instances, a party to litigation asks the court to appoint a receiver, although in some instances, the court can appoint a receiver without a request. This is rare.

A receiver is not the sheriff or marshal who is authorized to seize and sell property to satisfy a judgment, but a receiver might be directed to do those tasks under a court order. A receiver is not an advocate, like an attorney for each side, although the receiver can ask for independent judicial relief or seek an order, judgments, money awards, and other relief. A receiver is not a judge who makes decisions that bind parties, but a receiver does make many decisions, which can be affirmed by the court. A receiver is an independent person who answers primarily to the judge.

The core function of a receiver is to sell assets, which might include real estate, equipment, inventory, liquor licenses, or other valuable licenses or certificates. Under *Ager vs. Murray* (1881) 105 U.S. 126 and its progeny, a receiver, not the sheriff, can sell a patent, copyright, or trademark. In a digital world, judgment creditors seek the appointment of a receiver to sell valuable trademarks, including, for instance, the historic battle over sex. com. Banks and finance companies routinely seek the appointment of a receiver to run the business of a defaulted debtor, which includes collecting accounts receivable, recovering funds in bank account, or conducting a "going out of business sale."

A receiver can incur debts and liabilities in administration of the estate but bear no personal liability. After the receiver's performs the required duties, the receiver will move the court for an order to discharge the receiver of any potential liability, exonerate the receiver's bond, and distribute the property under the control of the receiver.

Many receivers are bankruptcy trustees. Some receivers are attorneys. Most receivers are professionals; the bulk of their careers is receivership, assignment, conservatorship, and other trust work. Many receivers are accountants or have long careers in the management of property of another. All receivers must be very good accountants because their first and primary responsibility is to account for the property that comes into their possession. Professional receivers belong to one or more receivership, insolvency, or bankruptcy associations. While trustees and assignees serve the interest of creditors, a receiver serves the interests of the persons designated in the order appointing the receiver.

A statutory dissolution of a corporation or limited liability company generally provides for payment to creditors. A creditor has a statutory right to sue shareholders or members who received assets of the dissolved entity. This is not a form of receivership but a "stand alone" right, which a creditor can seek to enforce. Creditors can chase down shareholders, insiders, and officers for illicitly taking corporate property under the Uniform Fraudulent

Transfer Act (UFTA) or breach of fiduciary claims. Most state corporation codes enable a judgment creditor to recover an unlawful dividend received by a shareholder, officer, director, or insider. These proceedings are akin to an insolvency because the corporation has stopped functioning, which enables the insiders to pick the corporate carcass clean.

Why Is a Receiver Appointed?

Receivers come in many flavors. Here are a few common examples:

The partners in partnership are unable to agree in the operation of a business. Or, similarly, husband and wife clash in the operation of a business. Or corporate shareholders and officers clash in the operation of a business. Upon application of a warring party, the court will appoint a receiver to manage and preserve the business. At the end of the case, the court orders the receiver to sell or liquidate the business. In some, but not all, cases, the court might order the receiver to pay trade bills.

A owner of an apartment building, shopping complex, farm, industrial property, or other property that houses businesses or tenants fails to pay the senior lender. The lender applies to the court for the appointment of a receiver to manage the property for the purpose of protecting the collateral, paying expenses, safeguarding the tenants or other interested persons, and attempting to rehabilitate the property in the face of a foreclosure sale.

A debtor who borrowed money from a lender who took a security interest in inventory, accounts, accounts receivable, bank accounts, rolling stock, and other personal property might default. The debtor would seek the appointment of a receiver to liquidate the inventory, collect the receivable, cash out the bank accounts, and sell any remaining collateral.

Courts also might appoint a receiver at the request of the U.S. government (Department of Justice, Securities and Exchange Commission (SEC), etc.), a state (or its agencies), a county, or a city to take control over businesses, financial institutions, stock brokerages, etc. with the obligation to protect, safeguard, or marshal assets; oust current owners; or manage a failing health care facility, convalescent hospital, acute care facility, rest home, or other facilities. The SEC routinely seeks the appointment of a receiver to take control over a failing, or fraud plagued, securities brokerage. Counties and cities frequently seek the appointment of a receiver to supervise renovation, rehabilitation, or demolition of buildings—particularly apartment buildings that are out of code compliance, an immediate danger to the community, or rife with permit violations.

Judgment creditors seek the appointment of a receiver to liquidate a debtor's business or sell assets, including patents, copyrights, trademarks, domain names, and other intangibles that typically a sheriff cannot sell. A judgment creditor might move the court to appoint a receiver, for example, to sell a liquor license, profitable lease, or other assets for which a receiver is more suitable than a sheriff. In the enforcement of a judgment, receivers frequently sell no residential real estate. Receivers, at the request of a judgment creditor, have run law offices, medical practices, hotels, restaurants, and even night clubs.

Receivers might take possession of property that was fraudulently conveyed, provide for its management, and sell the property for the benefit of the creditor. Once property has been recovered, the receiver can take charge, rehabilitate the property, and provide for its orderly sale. More than once, the court in a single order has unwound the fraudulent conveyance of real estate and appointed a receiver to take immediate charge.

Absent the most extreme circumstance, unsecured creditors cannot seek the appointment of a receiver. However, three creditors can push a debtor into an involuntary bankruptcy under Bankruptcy Code Section 303(a).

Receivers are appointed to carry out a judgment that provides for specific enforcement in the sale of real estate, recovery of assets, unwinding a transaction, or ousting party or third person from real property by virtue of an unlawful detainer action. Receivers have been appointed to take possession and control where a corporation has been dissolved, is insolvent, or is in imminent danger of insolvency, forfeiting its corporate rights.

This section outlined typical receivers, but the concept of receivership is very old. Over the last thousand years, receivers have been appointed for myriad reasons.

What Is the Role of the Debtor in the Appointment of a Receiver?

Resistor. In 90% of cases, a receiver is appointed over the objection of the debtor. Absent an involuntary bankruptcy proceedings, debtors choose to file a bankruptcy petition because bankruptcy offers a debtor the stay, a discharge of debts, and efficient liquidation of assets, among other remedies.

The purpose of bankruptcy is provide the debtor with a fresh start. An assignment offers to maximize the recovery to creditors, given its informality and freedom from expensive judicial oversight, and only the debtor can execute an assignment. Akin to an assignment, only the debtor (as the seller) and the buyer can proceed with bulk sales.

Barring the most unusual events, a debtor never seeks the appointment of a receiver. A receivership means the debtor is losing control over the property and income; moreover, the debtor is paying for the receiver as part of a loan expense or charge against the property. If the creditors are hounding the debtor, the debtor typically files Chapter 11, which enables the debtor to manage and control the business under the court's supervision. (The court might convert the Chapter 11 to Chapter 7, but the creditors would have to show good cause.)

A receiver is a remedy available to secured and trade creditors, the government, law enforcement, co-owners, and spouses. In most of the cases, a secured creditor seeks the appointment of a receiver to protect collateral. The debtor generally resists the receiver because the debtor is liable for the costs, fees, and expenses of the receiver. These expenses include the costs, fees, and expenses of the receiver, the receiver's accountant, and the receiver's attorney.

If the receiver is appointed to manage, care for, and liquidate collateral, the receiver is an expense that burdens the collateral, which is a fancy way of saying that the debtor pays for the receiver. If the business is failing, or the partners or other owners are in conflict, one partner usually seeks the appointment of a receiver over the objection of the other owner. Governments seek the appointment for failing businesses when the public is at risk. The owners routinely resist.

While occasionally a debtor might stipulate the appointment of a receiver sought by a lender, creditor, government, partner, or shareholder, rarely, if ever, would a debtor seek the appointment of a receiver. Receivers typically charge anywhere between $300.00 to $800.00 an hour. A receiver retains counsel who charges about the same. Receiver fees and charges from any modest case easily equal or exceed $50,000 and might break $100,000 without too much effort.

A receiver enables the creditor to oust the debtor from the asset or business and install a professional to dispose of the assets. Sometimes, but not often, a receiver might liquidate the business and provide for payment of creditors. This is unusual unless the state is looking to liquidate a business.

An Equity Receiver Is a Lien Creditor

Commercial Code Section 9102(b)(52) bestows lien creditor status upon an equity receiver. Are we done? Is this enough explanation? No, I am sorry to tell you, because an "equity receiver" is not a term defined by the UCC.

A lien creditor, like a trustee and assignee, takes priority over junior lien creditors, which includes those with a later filed financing statement (UCC). A lien creditor beats out an unperfected security interest. A lien creditor trumps the general unsecured creditors. Whether one receiver or another is a equity creditor, of course, is a different matter.

A Receiver Is the Mercedes "E" Class of the Law

Receivers are very expensive. They chew up lots of money. As mentioned, the usual is about $500.00 an hour. They hire attorneys who typically charge $500.00 an hour. Nothing is cheap in a receivership; costs routinely hit tens of thousands of dollars.

The reality is that only the wealthy can afford a receiver in commercial cases. The most common receivership involves taking possession of the debtor's property for very specific purposes, including foreclosure under a security interest or deed of trust (mortgaged property). Secured creditors routinely seek the appointment of a receiver to manage their real property collateral, which might consist of apartment buildings, farms, industrial or commercial businesses, and other fragile operations. While an officer of the court, operating under a very tight court order, the receiver in aid of foreclosure is an agent for the secured creditor and works hard to preserve the collateral. Under the order, the receiver has taken custody and control of the collateral. Absent extreme circumstances, the receiver does not accept, nor pay, the debtor pre-appointment claims because the role of the receiver is manage the collateral pending a foreclosure.

In some cases, at the conclusion of the receivership, the bank, as the lender, proceeds with a non judicial foreclosure of the real property. Banks are the number one consumers of receivers.

Pre-Receivership Claims Are Rarely, if Ever, Paid from the Estate

Absent an provision in the receivership order, the receiver has no duty to pay the debtor's pre-petition claims. Receivers are the agents of the court to fulfill the terms of a court order that meets the needs of the litigants. Mind you, some receivers will pay key vendors, such as the utilities, landlord, key trade vendors, certain key employees, and other expenses necessary to operate a business or maintain the collateral.

Trade creditors can grip but they cannot sue the receiver. In fact, the receiver is "sue proof," which means that creditors, third parties, and others need leave of court to sue the receiver. This is called the *Barton Doctrine* from the U.S. Supreme Court case in which the court stated: "It is a general rule that before suit is brought against a receiver leave of the court by which he was appointed must be obtained. *Davis* v. *Gray*, 16 Wall. 203, and the cases there cited" (*Barton v. Barbour*, 104 U.S. 126, 127, 26 L. Ed. 672 (1881)). Suing the receiver or garnishing the receiver is an act of contempt because the property in the hands of the receiver is deemed property in the hands of court. This is still good law (e.g., the *Barton Doctrine* was cited several times in 2015).

Is the Receiver Liable for the Claims that Arose during the Administration of the Estate?

Is this question getting too deep in the weeds? Not really. The courts appoint a receiver because the debtor defaulted on secured debt, mismanaged a business, or jeopardized the welfare of someone or someone's property. Most folks who find themselves subject to a receiver have mismanaged their businesses. As a result, the receiver is going to run a failing or troubled business. Absent a big cash deposit or guaranties of payment from the plaintiff who sought the appointment of a receiver, the receiver might well run up trade and commercial debt in the operation of the debtor's business. In dealing with receivers, most vendors only provide goods or services on C.O.D. basis, or they demand a letter of creditor, bond, deposit, or cash in advance. Some vendors demand a guaranty from the plaintiff. This is more than good credit management; it is a necessity because the order appointing the receiver exonerates the receiver of personal liability for the debts that might accrue during the administration of the estate. Utilities are experts in securing payment in advance of charges that accrue during a receivership. For everyone else, dealing with a receiver takes some time and effort to insure payment of administrative expenses.

At the conclusion of the case, the receiver files a motion for an order ratifying and approving the conduct of the receiver; approving and authorizing all accounts, including any receipts and disbursements; discharging the receiver of any liability; and exonerating the bonds. The administration creditor can oppose the motion and seek to surcharge the receiver for the trade debt or, alternatively, surcharge the collateral or even the secured creditor the trade debt. In some case, the creditor can seek payment under the bond. This motion is the best venue and, in many cases, the only venue to generate payment due administrative creditors. Experienced administrative creditors, such as utilities, might establish a separate receiver account but demand (and receive) a large deposit, surety bond, or guaranty by the creditor seeking the receiver.

Is There Any Mechanism for Payment to Pre-Receivership Creditors?

Yes and no.

No, because the short answer is unlikely given that an aggrieved party seeks the appointment of a receiver to vindicate the party's own rights. Receivership over marital property, a partnership, a failing corporation, or a general receivership that takes possession of property based on the conflict of owners might offer payment to creditors. However, payment to trade and commercial creditors is not required by law. Receivers serve the interest of the aggrieved parties who might or might not choose to pay creditors. At the conclusion of a case, the receiver is discharged, and the court orders the division of the assets to the parties, or sale, or other disposition. Trade creditors might (or might not) have a right of action against the debtor entity, who in most cases, is dead and gone—or its assets have been transferred to the warring factions.

Worse, if one judgment scores the appointment of a receiver to satisfy that judgment creditor's judgment, all of the other judgments creditor are ousted as a matter of law unless the other judgment creditors recorded (or filed) earlier liens. In the enforcement of judgment, the judgment who collects is the judgment creditor who wins the race to the courthouse. First to file is first to collect, and everyone else is a bystander.

Yes, because the courts routinely appoint a receiver to wind up the affairs of a failing business that owes money to trade vendors, the utilities, a landlord, taxing authorities, wage claimants, customers (for refunds and warranty work), and judgment creditors. These cases raise from corporation dissolutions at the hands of insiders, warring partners or spouses, or aggrieved creditors. This is a provisional "yes" because when a business edges toward a financial abyss, attorneys for all sides contemplate whether bankruptcy offers a more advantageous venue (i.e., is debtor friendly). Bankruptcy offers the right of a claw-back (i.e., preference or fraudulent conveyance) to return funds taken by insiders. Bankruptcy avoids unperfected or late perfected liens.

Federal, state, and county prosecutors push Ponzi operations, pyramid markets, and other criminal enterprises into a receivership. The receiver seeks to marshal and safeguard any remaining assets, seeks to recover any property in the hands of the wrongdoer, and ultimately offers a fund to the victims of the scheme. The receiverships are few and far between because bankruptcy provides a more effective forum; the trustee has greater power to claw back preferences and fraudulent conveyances. The bankruptcy court (and the bankruptcy code) offers the trustee, as opposed to a receiver, a more specialized forum and ease of administration that includes professional claim management through a claim administrator, transparent (i.e., PACER) proceedings, and decades of experience (i.e., *Madoff*, etc.).

In some limited cases, the parties can agree that the receiver is authorized to pay creditors and establish some type of claims filing program, approval, and payment in full or pro rata. Nothing under rules of equity compels payment, but if the debtor entity is solvent yet facing liabilities, then the parties, court, and receiver might agree to provide a mechanism to insure payment to creditors from asset estates.

What Are the Differences between a Receiver and a Bankruptcy Trustee, Assignee, or Bulk Sale?

A receiver is the agent of the court to carry out the duties specified by a judge at the request of private parties, the government, or in the public interest. A receiver typically has no obligation to pay the creditors of the debtor unless part of the order. A bankruptcy trustee is appointed by the bankruptcy judge to fulfill statutory duties that include payment to creditors from available funds after payment of other claims with a higher priority. Unlike a receiver, the bankruptcy trustee can recover preference, set aside fraudulent conveyance, avoid late filed liens, and easily investigate fraudulent conduct. (See Chapter 9 for more about bankruptcy.)

An assignee is the initial agent of the debtor to take possession and control of the debtor's assets. Upon acceptance, title to the assets passes to the assignee, who is now the trustee on behalf of the creditors and, like a trustee, will pay creditors after payment of other claims with a high priority. (See Chapter 10 for more about assignments.)

A bulk sale is statutory mechanism in which the seller deposits the title and the buyer deposits cash with a third party. Upon expiration of the 12 days, title passes to the buyer, and the cash is distributed to the creditors who have timely filed a creditor's claim. (See Chapter 11 for more about bulk transfers.)

Our next chapter moves on to a few types of funds for specific situations of loss or wrongdoing: statutory funds, bonds, and mass tort funds.

15

Statutory Funds, Bonds, and Mass Tort Funds

When a business fails, bankruptcy offers some recompense to creditors when the debtor is not stone cold dead. What happens when the debtor really rides off the rails? If bankruptcy is a version of Humpty Dumpty's great fall, a mega catastrophe leaves no pieces to even try to put together again; little to nothing remains for present and future creditors. What about a major company that files bankruptcy in the face of mass torts (e.g., asbestos, silicone breast implants, intrauterine devices)? Granted the company files a Chapter 11, and bankruptcy rules apply, but the outcomes are beyond normal expectations. These are each unique insolvency cases, so the rules and expectations are different.

Let's begin by looking at statutory funds or bonds due victims of licensees, permit holders, and certificate holders.

Statutory Funds

State governments provide statutory funds to compensate members of the general public who have been injured at the hands of a licensee or other business operator.

These are the usual funds:

- Real Estate Recovery Funds (Department of Real Estate)
- Client Security Funds (State Bar or State Attorney General)
- Workers' Compensation Uninsured Funds (CA: Uninsured Employers Benefits Trust Fund (UEBTF); NY: Uninsured Employers Fund (UEF))
- Victims of Crime Funds (Attorney General or Department of Justice of the relevant state)
- Victims of Corporate Fraud and Compensation Funds (Secretary of State, Department of Corporation or Business Oversight)

These funds offer victims compensation based on the timely filing of a claim, proof that the claim is covered by the fund's rules, and adjudication (i.e., verifiable proof of loss). Some of these funds have a cap on the amount of payments. Some claims compensate victims based on embezzlement suffered by the client (Real Estate Recovery and Client Security Funds). The victim funds are based on theft, personal injury, or other tangible losses suffered by victims of violent crimes or property damage. Some of these funds step into the shoes of an insurer if, for example, the employer lacked insurance and did not obtain an exemption for self-insurance (i.e., workers' compensation).

These funds benefit the victim and not the person who was responsible for the loss. To summarize a broad swatch of the law, these entities compensate the victim for their loss at the hands of the wrongdoer. The fund (usually a state agency) compensates the victim and can seek civil recourse against the wrongdoer or third parties. For example, the agencies in charge of the Uninsured Workers' Compensation funds have a right to proceed against an underlying tortfeasor (i.e., the person who caused the accident) or even the employer (should the employee file suit against the employer).

The state agencies have departments dedicated to processing these claims filed by consumers or members of the statutorily protected class. These agencies have likewise issued very detailed rules, which are online or otherwise readily available. These rules are important because they provide a very detailed roadmap toward compensation. These claims are time sensitive. Most claimants hire a competent and experienced attorney.

Uninsured workers' compensation funds provide substitute workers' compensation benefits due the employee whose employer failed to obtain workers' compensation insurance. These claims can amount to millions, depending upon the severity of the injury or even death. Serious injuries might require medical care for months, years, or decades and can include long term disability and medical benefits. An employer who fails to obtain workers' compensation insurance commits a major civil and criminal crime.

In some cases and depending on the state, these funds require the claimant to exhaust all civil remedies, which include filing suit, obtaining judgment, and pursuing collection of the case until bankruptcy or proof that the debtor is judgment proof. On the other hand, some funds will pay upon presentment of the proof of loss, after, of course, the exercise of due diligence. In all cases, the time to file the claim is set by statute or rules. This is very important. Time waits for no one when it comes to filing a claim.

Upon payment, the claimant transfers the claim to the fund through subrogation. In nearly all cases, the claimant does not care because the fund is the sole source of payment. In effect, the claimant is selling the claim to the fund in exchange for payment. On the other hand, but infrequently, the debtor has assets that the claimant might want to reach. This is rare, but not improbable, given the rising real estate values post meltdown. If the claimant obtains judgment, the funds might demand an assignment of the judgment for the purpose of enforcement.

Bonds and Deposits

Bonds and deposits are a very big deal and common in many professions. If a licensee causes some type of loss or harm that leads to compensable loss, in many cases the licensee is financially impecunious, which is a fancy word for 'flat broke.' The bond or state funds might be the sole source for ready payment. Federal and state licensing law mandates the posting of a bond to enable consumers of the licensee's service an opportunity to recover their losses.

The poster persons for bonds are contractors. Bonds are common, and the amount of a bond is usually around $10,000.00, more or less. This small amount should not deter the claimant, whose loss might be six figures, because the bond fund might be the sole recourse for payment of the loss. More than one miscreant has "fled the scene," which means that the claimant's sole recourse is the bond.

Bonds are "pro consumer" in assuring payment on behalf of the aggrieved customer. State and federal law condition the posting of a bond as a condition of issuing a license. These are the most common bonds:

- Notaries public
- All contractors
- All moving and transportation entities (consumer and commercial)
- Process servers
- Auctioneers or auction houses
- Pest control operators
- Collection agencies (depending on the state)
- Warehouse and cold storage operators
- Most insurance brokers or third parties handling funds or properties of another
- Self insured employers (employers who do not have workers' compensation insurance, but self insure)

The list of businesses that are bonded goes on: credit service companies, dance studios, discount buying organizations, employment agencies, foreclosure consultants, health studios, immigration consultants, invention developers, job listing agencies, nurses' registries, travel agents, and many others. Federal agencies require bonds, including the Federal Maritime

Agency for freight forwarders and related entities. If an entity is licensed, the entity is probably bonded. Depending on the state, most licensed persons are bonded. Many businesses tout claims of "bonded and insured." Whether these claims are true is a challenge to discern.

In conservatorships, receiverships, probates, trusts, and other fiduciary proceedings, the court imposes a bond requirement equal to the amount of funds maintained by the estate professional.

Bonds are posted in nearly all major construction projects. These bonds include performance bonds, payment bonds, mechanics lien release bonds, surety bonds, and bonds demanded by governmental entities. This is a very short list of bonds that proliferate in construction. All government projects require bonds.

Bonds are posted as a condition of the issuance of writs of attachment, temporary restraining orders, third party claim practice, preliminary injunctions, and other provisional relief. Third party custodians holding funds for parties are bonded. This is another short list that is illustrative but not comprehensive.

A claim under a bond requires a written demand, verified proof of loss, and proof that the loss arose under the terms of the bond. Depending upon the bond and the amount of loss, the bonding company can demand significant documentation to support the loss. Depending upon the state, payment under the contractor's bond might have to arise from the contracting services of the licensee as opposed to nonpayment of any obligation (i.e., spousal support). The bonding company can accept or reject the claim. In some, but not all cases, the bond amounts range from $5,000 to $25,000, which might be a pittance of the total loss, particularly in claims against contractors and moving companies. Some bonding companies will pay on a claim, while other bonding companies will only pay on a judgment. This varies from state to state.

A claim against a bonding company, if paid, results in the suspension or cancellation of the license. The state requires as a condition of licensing that the licensee have a valid bond on file. If the bond is pulled off the shelf, the state suspends or cancels the license. An unlicensed person cannot collect in any judicial proceedings, which destroys the contractor's ability to earn a decent living. Any money paid to an unlicensed contractor is subject to recovery by the aggrieved property owners. Many licensees, when faced with a claim against the bond, are highly motivated to settle with the claimant. The fact that the licensee fails to settle with the claimant is strong evidence that the licensee is in the midst of a financial (or personal) death spiral.

Like state funds, the bonding company is subrogated to the claim of the claimant. Similarly, the fact of subrogation would not prejudice the claimant because in most cases, the bond is sole recourse to any payment. A licensee who lets a dispute spiral into a judgment for misconduct is probably headed out the door anyway. Expect multiple claims against the licensee, which would render the bond insolvent, which means that the dollar value of the claims exceed the face value of the bond. Multiple claims upon the bond can result upon pro rata distribution or distribution that is first come, first served. If the first person is paid from the bond, the second person is kicked to the bond curb. A claimant should file as soon as possible.

Nearly every state requires auto insurance. Taxi cab companies, among other high volume transportation companies, post a bond with the DMV in the amount equal to the minimum for auto insurance.

Mass Tort Funds: Mega Bankruptcies

Asbestos has caused millions of deaths and life threatening disabilities. Dalkon Shield intrauterine devices crippled thousands of women. Silicon breast implants have ruined many lives. These defective products drove the manufacturers (and others along the distribution line) into mega Chapter 11s. These are all hundred million or billion dollar bankruptcies that span in excess of 20 years. These cases are the apex of insolvency when we compare the billion dollar portfolio of large dollar claims to the finite and limited assets. The most famous case is of Johns Manville, a company that used asbestos to manufacture roofing, insulation, and other products, which filed bankruptcy in 1982. In 1988 as part of the bankruptcy plan of reorganization, the court approved the Manville Trust, which is still functioning.

These Chapter 11s culminate in a confirmed plan of reorganization, which provides that the debtor's insurance policies are paid into a post confirmation trust; that revested debtor, a public entity, issues a large percentage of its newly issued stock to the trust and pays in a portion of its profits for many years into the trust. The creditors, which are the tort victims, file their claims with the claims agent or, post confirmation, with the trust itself. These trust funds control a large, multi-million dollar portfolio of assets. The plan and ensuing trusts offer the tort victim a rigid set of rules by which (and by when) to file claims. The buzzword is that these mega plans "channel" the tort claims away from the courts and into trust administration.

This is a short summary of a topic that includes hundreds of scholarly and academic treatments. What to do is easy: Follow the rules in timely filing a claim. Be prepared to support the claim at the level of proof in a civil trial.

16

Conclusion

The risk of insolvency offers many lessons. The first lesson is that any big customer or big vendor might become insolvent. One day, the customer does not pay its outstanding balance or the vendor fails to deliver key inventory. The client, a creditor or purchaser, is placed at risk.

Counsel for a creditor or a buyer embraces insolvency as an eternal looming threat. The General Motors bankruptcy provides an example of how this can lead to a ripple effect: Many of its key suppliers likewise filed bankruptcy. This can happen in either direction: When a major supplier of key components goes out of business, its big customers stop shipping their product to their customers, which creates another ripple effect.

Counsel has many lines of defense to protect a client from the repercussions arising from a customer or vendor collapse:

A. Insert security interest in all contracts, invoices, credit applications, and the terms and conditions of anything.

B. Negotiate for personal guaranties that are drafted with standard disclaimers.

C. Establish a credit regime that minimizes losses.

D. If the customer defaults, quickly seek to invoke rights to suspend performance or reclaim goods. These are the best remedies under difficult circumstances.

E. If the parties enter into a payment program, secure the payment program with a security interest and personal guaranty; ratify and confirm the amount of the debt; waive set-offs, jury trial rights, and any other putative defenses.

F. In filing suit, seek a pre-judgment of attachment or claim and delivery (replevin) at the earliest opportunity in an attempt to reach the assets of the debtor outside the 90-day claw-back period.

G. If the customer (or vendor) files bankruptcy, makes an assignment for the benefit of creditors, or proceeds down another insolvency path, file a proof of claim, request special notice, and "bird dog" every piece of paper that the courts or the parties generate.

H. Research and provide accurate estimations of probable outcomes. For example, because bankruptcy and assignments implicate the rights of the trustee (or debtor in possession) or the assignee for the benefit of creditors as "lien holders" under the law, the creditor's security interest, if not perfected, might become junior to the claims of the trustee or assignee. The creditor (or buyer, if the vendor filed) should have modest expectation of what the insolvency might generate and seriously study whether further proceedings are warranted in insolvency.

Insolvency is a fact of life. In many business lives, insolvency never appears over the horizon. Business people pay their bills and pay on time. Yet sometimes businesses default, leaving creditors, vendors, employees, and taxing authorities "high and dry."

Counsel needs to anticipate this risk at the outset of each relationship by inserting pro-active terms that will convert the seller of products or services into a secured creditor. Should the buyer default, be prepared to exercise UCC remedies: Use suspension and reclamation. Without delay, file suit and attach. And, when all else fails, file the claim and work towards a recovery.

Index